D0872993

GREAT COMMISSION ADVENTURES

Great Commission Adventures: Real-Life Encounters of an Unlikely Missionary
by Rebecca Friday • Copyright © 2022 Rebecca Friday

ISBN: 978-1-946497-92-5 • Library of Congress Control Number: 2022943248

Theological Editor, Ronald W. Kirk

Managing Editor, Design, Michelle Shelfer, benediction.biz

Proofreader, Nikola Dimitrov

Photos are from the author's collection. Illustrations are from Wikimedia Commons, PD. Photo of Honduran protests is from HCH Televisión Digital.

Printed in the US by Custom Printing.

Ventura, California
805-642-2070 • 805-276-5129

CIPA
CHRISTIAN INDIE
PUBLISHING
ASSOCIATION

GREAT COMMISSION ADVENTURES

REAL-LIFE ENCOUNTERS
OF AN UNLIKELY MISSIONARY

Rebecca Friday

The Gail Grace Nordskog Collection

VENTURA, CALIFORNIA

DEDICATION

For my children and grandchildren, with the prayer that they will wholeheartedly love and obey the Lord Jesus Christ all the days of their lives.

CONTENTS

ACKNOWLEDGMENTS

I WOULD LIKE TO EXPRESS MY APPRECIATION TO THE PEOPLE behind the scenes at Nordskog Publishing for their dedication to advancing the Kingdom of God on earth and for believing that this book has something worthwhile to say about the Great Commission. They have sacrificially used their home and their business to magnify the Lord. I am blessed to be their friend and sister in the faith.

I'm also thankful to Ronald W. Kirk, Theological Editor, and Michelle Shelfer, Managing Editor at Nordskog Publishing. They doubled the value of my message, not only with their editing expertise but by challenging me to be a forthcoming and courageous wordsmith.

Additionally, my husband deserves credit for being my biggest fan throughout the writing of this book and for reading every page more than once.

Lastly, a shout-out to my old friend, Susan Miller, who believed from the beginning that I could successfully author this book, something neither of us would have imagined possible back in middle school, before the blood of Jesus forever changed our lives. I can't wait to be her best friend in heaven, where wheelchairs are absolutely unnecessary.

REBECCA FRIDAY

FOREWORD

One summer, my friend Andrae asked me to pick up some snorkel gear from Rebecca Friday's home. I really didn't have time since we were leaving for Hondurus the next day, but I agreed to help him out.

I thought I'd be quick. Get to "Mrs. Friday's" (as Andrae affectionately referred to her) house, grab the goods, and get back to pack. But, as soon as Rebecca opened the door, something just clicked. She invited me in, and we sat on her couch overlooking the bay, ate chips, and chatted it up!

I'm not sure exactly how long I was there that day, but I do know it was the start of yet another "Great Commission adventure." Our God is so cool like that—what a treat He gave me, simply because I was willing to do a favor for a friend!

I'd been on many mission trips before this one, and even to this same orphanage, but you're never the same after being there with Rebecca Friday. You see, the houseparents at this particular children's home leave the country for two weeks every year, and Rebecca Friday was given the *giant* task of filling their shoes. She took on the role like a champ year after year.

She had a chart, stickers, prizes, games, and all kinds of activities the kids had come to expect and look forward to. Rebecca even brought special treats for the staff—each one personal—things that could only be purchased stateside.

Rebecca once told me that she wore eight layers of clothes on her long, hot flight over to Honduras so she would have room to bring those special goodies in her suitcase.

In the pages of this book, you'll get to experience what life is like when on a Great Commission adventure. It is written by hands that have nurtured, loved, cooked, cleaned, cried, hugged, put bandaids on, made tortillas with, prayed for, and loved like Jesus.

Rebecca humbly recalls memories from year after year—always giving credit where credit is due: to the Lord Jesus Christ. She uses Scripture and well-told, detailed stories to encourage the reader. She challenges us all, like Jesus Himself does, to Great Commission work. At the end of each chapter are a few concise thoughts as well as questions to get us all really thinking.

I'm a foster mom. My husband and I have fostered well over one hundred children. We often ponder why we were born to the wonderful parents we have, while the kids we care for were not, just like the kids you're going to read about. Why were they born drug-exposed or to abusive families? Any one of us could have had neglectful parents, and yet most of us were not only spared that but given parents that adored us.

While we haven't come up with the answer and likely won't until eternity, we do know that "to whom much has been given, much will be required"(Luke 12:48).

We get asked a lot of questions about why we foster, or why we use our vacation time to take care of others. Simply put, it's what Jesus did for us! Not everyone is called to foster or to travel overseas to serve, but *everyone* is called to do *something*. James 1:27 (NIV) instructs us all:

> *Religion that God our Father accepts as pure and faultless is this: to look after orphans and widows in their distress and to keep oneself from being polluted by the world.*

Don't buy into the empty wisdom of the world that we need to put ourselves first. That will never bring true lasting joy. My dad was a Baptist pastor. He taught many truths from the Bible, but one of my favorite things he modeled for us was to always be generous. I've found that you're never happier than when you're serving someone else.

Rebecca shares some practical—plus some hilarious and not-so-practical—ways that she helped countless kids and adults. Take some tips from her!

Buckle up. Turn the pages to read about God-sized miracles only He can do, through a willing servant named Rebecca Friday.

KRISTEN WISE
Multi-award-winning film producer

MY MISSIONARY FRIEND, REBECCA

$\mathcal{M}$y dear friend Rebecca Friday has inspired me for years with her longtime commitment to "visit and look after the fatherless," as James admonishes us in James 1:27—in Rebecca's case referring to the orphans of Central America. I have watched over the years as God has utilized Rebecca's missionary work not only to improve the lives of orphans but also to sanctify her. We who follow Jesus surrender ourselves to a process by which God conforms us day by day, little by little, to the image of His Son. This is called our sanctification. Difficult as that is, we steadily learn self-sacrifice and develop the fruits of the Spirit—love, joy, peace, patience, kindness, goodness, faithfulness, gentleness, and self-control. Rebecca presents a beautiful example of a fruitful, sanctified servant of God.

Rebecca's preparations for her missions trips say so much about her Christian walk. These times of preparation are not just about shopping and packing. They are times of deep spiritual tempering, during which she puts on the full armor of God and tunes her spiritual ears to hear the voice of her Shepherd, without whom she cannot effectively serve. She can't imagine going on these trips without God and His protection. Her missionary work and her whole life thus reflect the blessing that comes from deep dependence on God. You'll see what I mean when you read her stories.

God is a missionary God, and He sends people out on missions for His glory. Friday calls herself "an unlikely missionary." Maybe everyone surrendered to God's will in the furtherance of the Gospel of Jesus Christ has sometimes felt "unlikely." I know I have. I am far too aware of my failings to consider myself anything but unlikely. We all, saved by grace, are unlikely candidates for contributing to His awesome drama of redemption. We must come away from times of dedicated service to God with a keen awareness of our powerlessness and God's limitless power. We're left marveling at Him. He gets all the glory. We are weak so He can be strong.

Let my friend Rebecca and her God-honoring life inspire you to be bold in bringing the love of God to your own mission field, whether you are called to a faraway land or to those in your own household.

In this is love, not that we loved God, but that He loved us and sent His Son to be the propitiation for our sins. Beloved, if God so loved us, we also ought to love one another. (First John 4:10–11)

GAIL GRACE NORDSKOG
Co-publisher, Nordskog Publishing, Inc.

INTRODUCTION

*Now therefore, thus says the L*ORD *of hosts, "Consider your ways and*
thoughtfully reflect on your conduct!" (Haggai 1:5)

*R*emember the first time you fell madly in love? Remember
what you would have sacrificed for that person and what
you would have done to grow and perfect that relationship? God
wired us to crave extreme love so we would search for it with all
our hearts until discovering the flawless love that can only be found
in Jesus. Finding perfect love in the One who calls Himself Love
is the only way to permanently meet our deepest need, because
that relationship only depends on one perfect person, and that one
perfect person is Jesus.

Most people look for extreme love in humans, but all human
relationships fall short because humans love imperfectly. Still, we
become fooled and think we have found true and perfect love in
a mortal. After we fall in love with another human, it's natural to
want to tell others about our loved one.

God tells us in Matthew 28:19 that after we have found the perfect love of Jesus, we are supposed to tell others about our Loved
One. But sharing the love of Jesus is not natural. It's supernatural, and most Christians are reluctant to tell others about their
Beloved One. Human-to-human transmission of God's loving plan
of redemption is a miraculous thing, but the risk factor urges us to
hold back. Family and friends may hate you for telling them about
the love of Jesus. In some places of the world, people go to jail, and
some even die for telling others about their Loved One.

But remember your first love? You were ready to face death for the sake of that person, as we have seen in so many Hollywood productions. Should we not be willing to make that same sacrifice for the lover of our souls? God's spectacular love ought to compel us to take risks so that His Kingdom can come and His will can be done on earth as it is in Heaven.

Sharing God's reconciliation plan, achieved through the death, burial, and resurrection of Jesus, isn't easy or convenient to do with one person in your homeland. Leaving the homeland to share it with the world is a monumental task that takes courage and determination. The rocket launch onto the battlefield of missions only happens after believers move from virtual Christianity to Romans 12:1 living-sacrifice Christianity. That sort of surrender moves them beyond the tendency to play games with their faith commitment. Great Commission work is not a game. Missionaries are frontline warriors sent out to rescue a dying world.

After taking the plunge into Great Commission work, the Holy Spirit will open your eyes to an alternative world where the great God of the universe lowers Himself to touch your life and ministry in ways that are undeniable. It is faith-building when things become desperate and then God shows up to save the day. The alternative world of missions is like a battlefield between the forces of heaven and hell, where God intervenes in a powerful way, because without Him, hell prevails.

Life on the battlefield is difficult to explain to your Christian friends and family back home. Your unbelieving friends will think you need a therapist. You may even doubt yourself, and you may have to ask your Great Commission war buddies if things really happened as you remember. Sometimes, God's startling presence is an exclusive event that happens between just you and God—therefore, no other human will ever fully understand how heaven and earth intersected while you were on a Great Commission assignment.

The inexplicable world of Great Commission adventures may make you feel a bit like Dr. Indiana Jones. At first glance, Dr. Jones appears to be a boring college professor, but in his other life, he is living on the edge, experiencing high adventure and barely escaping disaster at every turn, as he scarcely holds on to his hat. Whenever I prepare for *my* other life as a Great Commission agent, I always pack a special hat to protect me from the harsh UV rays in the tropics. Labeled by the manufacturer as an "adventure hat," it has witnessed some serious and supernatural phenomena.

There is a scene in the movie *Indiana Jones and the Temple of Doom* that captures my typical reaction to the adventurous aspect of Great Commission work. The setting is a jungle suspension bridge above an expanse that is so deep and treacherous that it sucks all the oxygen out of your lungs. As opposing groups are traversing the bridge from opposite sides, there is a confrontation that becomes hostile. Swords are drawn with the threat of cutting the bridge apart. The situation escalates until reckless swords begin slicing the bridge asunder. A kid named Shorty tells the terrified woman on the bridge, "Hang on, Lady, we goin' for a ride," as everyone holds on for dear life!

Whenever I get into the car to leave for the airport on a Great Commission assignment, I feel a bit like the lady on the bridge. Great Commission adventure is never ordinary and not always safe or predictable. Everyone should go into it well informed of the possible outcomes and dangers.

The purpose of this book is to inspire and prepare missionaries and their support teams by highlighting the significance of the Great Commission and providing real-life stories, including stories of the perils and rewards of fieldwork. Although the narratives described took place in Latin America, the message has application to mission work in most of the world because of the commonality of corruption, injustice, and poverty.

I hope this book will provoke thought about the variety of ways to implement the Great Commission and also encourage all believers to carefully consider their contribution to the grand plan. Some of the typical ways of advancing the Kingdom of God are church planting, medical care, construction, and education. But there are many other ways to serve, such as water purification, music ministry, and aviation services. A young family in my church is preparing to leave for a country that is closed to Christian missionaries. The husband has been certified in advanced rock-climbing skills, which will be used to develop tourism in the destination country while simultaneously engaging in the Great Commission. The couple posts photos of the man hanging from sheer cliffs, which should keep their prayer supporters on their knees praying for his safety as well as the real reason he is risking life and limb for the Kingdom.

On the front lines, Great Commission work is a wild and thrilling adventure. What could be more phenomenal than God at work within you to advance His eternal Kingdom? As a serial short-term missionary, I've only participated in annual, bite-size chunks of the Great Commission. I admire those who have had the thrill of full-time, lifelong mission work. I would have loved a career as a Bible translator to an unreached people group.

> *The mission field is like a journey through an unmapped minefield. Putting on spiritual armor with an attitude of adventure is to the warrior's advantage.*

Certainly, the purpose of the Great Commission is *not* adventure, but framing fieldwork as adventure is a helpful antidote to discouragement and fatigue. The mission field is like a journey through an unmapped minefield. Putting on spiritual armor with an attitude of adventure is to the warrior's advantage, knowing that pushing back enemy lines comes with pain and sacrifice.

If you commit to frontline missions, expect adventure in epic proportions. Pray without ceasing and never allow the adventure to be eclipsed by inconvenience or frustration. Hang on to your hat and enjoy the wild ride.

Most of my missionary adventures have been in Honduras, but it is only one out of 195 countries for you to consider as a destination. Not everyone goes to the front lines, but for those who do, a dependable network of people for financial, emotional, logistical, and prayer support is necessary. In the book of Haggai, God twice admonishes us, "Now therefore, thus says the LORD of hosts, 'Consider your ways and thoughtfully reflect on your conduct!'" (Haggai 1:5, 7). As you do this, please give careful thought to *your* part in the Great Commission mandate. Any believer can contribute to Great Commission fulfillment in some way. A child can save coins to help finance a favorite missionary. A licensed driver can deliver Great Commission travelers to the airport. A ninety-year-old bedridden senior can pray for Great Commission workers who are on assignment in a distant land.

If you enjoy travel and can tolerate out-of-your-comfort-zone experiences, you may be a good candidate for the front lines. If you do go to the front lines, understand that fieldwork is fraught with obstacles, hazards, discomfort, and hardships. Simultaneously, it is also full of glorious purpose, with a rare glimpse of eternity that you will not find elsewhere. Testimonies of God showing up through miraculous interventions abound in Great Commission work.

The eternal perspective of the Great Commission is what motivates frontline missionaries to do that which looks absurd and counterproductive to an unbelieving world. The strong belief in what lies beyond the grave drives them to put away all the "good things in life" that usually consume the thoughts and energy of ordinary people. They take battlefield risks because they prioritize heaven over the here and now. They enlist in God's Special Forces because they know the end of the story and act accordingly. They are forward-thinking believers, stepping out in faith to become stakeholders in the grand enterprise of the Great Commission.

Special Forces have a different mindset than the rest of us who stay at home. Their Great Commission perspective is linear because it is rooted in eternity, instead of the cyclical perspective illustrated by the farmer who cycles annually from harvest to harvest. The individual assignments of missionaries are like pieces of a puzzle fit together on a continuum, where the completed whole will be far greater than the sum of its parts.

What we observe on this side of eternity is only a small part of the big picture of the Great Commission. Our lifespans limit us from seeing the end results of how God multiplies our seed planting to bring in the harvest of souls. No one can truly understand how or why God entrusts and then successfully uses His followers to accomplish the end result of the Great Commission. Heaven will be a revelation.

Before Jesus ascended into heaven, He entrusted his followers with the Great Commission. It was a command with a job description. The job description included the privilege of working with God in His rescue operation to populate heaven.

Let's pretend for a moment that a Fortune 500 company offered you a meaningful, well-rewarded job that you didn't deserve and weren't qualified to do, but they still wanted you to work for them. Wouldn't you say yes? The opportunity to be employed in the Great Commission is a far better job offer, with higher returns for your labor and longer-lasting benefits.

However, Great Commission work doesn't feel like a Fortune 500 job. It feels more like an impossible mission. The familiar recorded messages in the episodes and remakes of *Mission Impossible* illustrate an important point. Those messages describe an impossible mission and then add the same eight words: "Your mission, should you choose to accept it…" Likewise, with the Great Commission, you have a compelling choice to make. You don't *have to* obey the command—you don't even *have to* support the cause. You can ignore it altogether. God won't force your compliance. He doesn't need you and He doesn't need me. You don't *have to* be part of the Great Commission; you *get to* be part of the Great Commission. Walking away from becoming a stakeholder in the Great Commission when you have been called and equipped would be like Tom Cruise listening to his world-saving *Mission Impossible* opportunity and then saying, "Nah…not gonna do it. I'm just gonna stay at home and do something safe and ordinary."

It's not easy to understand why God would entrust believers with a mission that is impossible in human terms, especially considering its eternal outcome. But He does. Furthermore, the Bible makes the important point in Matthew 9:37 that there are only a few laborers who are willing to go forth into a world that desperately needs rescuing. This makes a commitment to the understaffed Great Commission an urgent and unique offer to consider.

The purpose of the Great Commission described in the Synoptic Gospels was given by the resurrected Christ. He commanded His disciples to leave their homeland to spread the Gospel worldwide until every nation received the message. The task was not completed in their lifetimes, so the baton has been passed on to subsequent generations.

I'll never forget the first summer that I took off on my first big Great Commission trip to Guatemala. It was not an easy entry point for a novice short-term missionary. While I was on assignment, I thought I was going to die. Instead of dying, I returned home and took five years off to recover and finish up seventeen units of college Spanish. I love the language and the people who speak it.

With my new and improved Spanish skills, I jumped back into short-term missions, with several trips to Belize and El Salvador. I've taken each of my children individually along with me on various assignments. I cherish the memories and heartily recommend this to parents.

The next time I left home for travel with a purpose was to the mainland of Honduras and then after that, the island of Roatán. When I first started doing short-term mission work, the plan was to travel to different locations, working my way south from Mexico through Central America and then on to South America. However, I never finished all the Central American countries because of my fondness for and connection with the children in the orphanages on the island of Roatán. It is the place where I stopped looking for the next new place to explore. It became my home away from home.

The island of Roatán has been a bittersweet place for me. I usually head for the island excited about seeing the children at the orphanages. However, I usually return home thinking I won't ever return to all that heartache. Working as a temporary orphanage director, I have had an insider's view into the sickening world of parental neglect and cruelty. It has been gut wrenching at times to be a first-hand observer of the pain and suffering of children who have been victimized by an evil parent. Some of the stories in this book were hard to put into words. Some of the details have been excluded because they are too dreadful to repeat. You may find the narratives intense because of the evil committed against children. Once, I was offered the opportunity to view evidence that documented abuse against children who were brought to the orphanage, but I didn't have the stomach for it.

All the stories in this book are true, but most of the names have been changed to protect the privacy of those who did not deserve to be orphaned or abused. Many of the stories will take you behind the scenes of Roatán's Caribbean tourist destinations, where there is an island populated mostly by people who live below the poverty level without a government safety net.

If you are thinking about a vacation in the Caribbean, please consider ministry opportunities on the Honduran island of Roatán. You could plan a vacation by cruise or flight and fill up any extra space in your luggage with items that are needed. (Visit roatanmission.com, clinicaesperanza.org or sblmroatan.net.) Or, after your arrival on the island, you could grab a taxi to the orphanage in Gravel Bay and find out what they need and then go shopping. As if Great Commission work weren't already enough of an adventure, there is a large thrift store at the Mega Plaza Mall in French Harbor where you could take the orphanage children shopping. Spoiler alert: some of the on-site people who work at these charitable organizations are more trustworthy than others, so monetary gifts are best given through the websites.

If you want to give until you bleed, you could do something completely crazy for Jesus, like opening up your heart and home to a teenager from one of the orphanages to attend high school and/or college in the United States on a study visa.

> *All missionaries have exciting books full of personal adventures within them that usually go unpublished.*

I have had so many out-of-this-world Great Commission adventures that I knew I could not take all the memories to my grave without first sharing them. All missionaries have exciting books full of personal adventures within them that usually go unpublished.

Hopefully, this book will encourage you to prayerfully consider a personal commitment to some active role in missions. I hope that as you read the chronicles of my Great Commission adventures, it will inspire some of you to grab your own adventure hats and take off for Timbuktu to "go therefore and make disciples of all the nations [help the people to learn of Me, believe in Me, and obey My words], baptizing them in the name of the Father and of the Son and of the Holy Spirit" (Matthew 28:19).

RUMINATIONS

I jumped into Great Commission work with the wrong motives. I grew up wanting to be an airline stewardess for the free flight pass. Mission work opened up the world of travel for me. What I didn't know was that the Great Commission is a life-or-death undertaking ordained by God with outcomes of eternal significance.

In the beginning, I didn't understand that mission work involved sacrifice and that everyone should sacrifice in some way to comply with Christ's commandment to spread the Gospel until the whole world knows about God's redemptive plan for mankind.

1. What is the Great Commission? Can the Great Commission sometimes be accomplished through domestic outreaches that seek to spread the Gospel and disciple those outside the faith while remaining at home? Also, are there opportunities to reach nonnationals that God has brought to your homeland?

2. Where do you fit in to the grand plan of the Great Commission, and what are your motives?

3. How have you risked a relationship for the purpose of sharing the Gospel with a friend or relative?

ONE

CHAOS IN TIJUANA

And so it is written,...that repentance [necessary] for forgiveness of sins would be preached in His name to all the nations, beginning from Jerusalem. (Luke 24:46–47)

WOMBAT is an acronym for *waste of money, brains, and time*. It seemed to me like a good description of my first attempt at Great Commission work. I was a volunteer on a one-day church bus trip to an orphanage in Tijuana, Mexico. Our church leaders were on a vision tour, checking out the possibility of an outreach to the orphanage. The volunteers were there to entertain the children. There wasn't much preparation for the trip. All we had to do was sign up and show up early on the appointed day so the bus could roll out of the church parking lot before the sun came up. We spent more time traveling on the bus and waiting at the border than we did with the children.

On the bus ride to our destination, some of the volunteers grumbled under their breath when the bus stopped at an In-N-Out Burger restaurant for lunch because they had no option other than red meat. When the bus stopped there again for dinner on the way home, you can imagine the reaction. Maybe the leaders thought they would be spiritually covered by In-N-Out's signature Bible verses printed on the paper goods, or maybe they really liked the hamburgers.

The orphanage was not far from our church, but it felt like we were on a different planet. It was shocking and pitiful to see the wooden structure that the children called home, or in this case, casa. It reminded me of my Aunt Gertie's barn in Wisconsin, only smaller in scale. The lumber of the wooden structure was so weathered that you could see tiny gaps where the wood once fit together, and you could feel wisps of wind when you were indoors. There was no indoor plumbing. The dirt floor was not what you might imagine, and at first, it seemed quaint. It was a slightly spongy, worn path, sealed and compacted by bare feet, which added a sheen to the top layer, so you could sweep loose debris out the front door. But dirt floors are extremely unsanitary because they are laden with soil-borne pathogens such as parasites and bacteria, which can cause disease and death, especially for children under five years old.

After we got beyond the earthiness of the house interior, we asked where the children slept. We learned that the living area doubled as a dormitory by night, with beds that were unrolled onto the floor. There was no upholstered furniture in the house, only rough-hewn wooden benches and narrow tables with the sharp ends of nails exposed in some places.

The hilly half-acre property that surrounded the children's home was a good match for the house. It was mostly hardened, cracked soil, unsuitable even for weeds, with broken glass scattered around the barren landscape. As a career public school teacher, I immediately wondered why there was no playground equipment. That's when I emerged from the stun-gun effect of my surroundings and realized that I was no longer in a culture of abundance, where people live like royalty and sometimes groan about having to eat red meat when they prefer poultry.

Inside the decrepit home, we played, laughed, sang, and prayed with the sweet children who had no parents. There is a quality about poor, unspoiled children that is inexplicably lovable. They were so grateful for all the love and attention that they made us a thank-you card with everyone's signature. But the brevity of the trip made it difficult to memorize everyone's name, let alone achieve any sort of significant bonding.

The day trip to Tijuana was a short and sweet blur. Pulling away in the bus, the excursion didn't feel very worthwhile. But it *was not* a waste of money, brains, and time. God doesn't waste Great Commission fieldwork—He enriches and multiplies it. For me, that first cross-cultural experience in Mexico was a valuable introduction to Latin America and the culture of scarcity. Additionally, orphanage ministry began to quietly tug at my heart. The trip was a launchpad for my career as a serial short-term missionary to other parts of Latin America, mostly to orphans.

A few years later, I was off to Tijuana for a second time during Easter vacation with my son's high school youth group. The youth pastor was under fire from the "helicopter parents" in the church because of his lack of prudence and his hesitancy about parental involvement. I loved Tom's authenticity, but I understood the parents' concerns after serving as a chaperone on the trip.

In some ways, Tom was a youth leader extraordinaire; but he had not yet found his niche in ministry. He was adventurous and fun, and he loved the Lord. He was skilled at preparing his students for Great Commission ministry and wanted all of us to push the bounds of whatever we thought were our limitations. He also knew the importance of prayer and evangelism.

Tom asked me to translate during the training. I told him that I couldn't because I was only about 20 percent fluent in Spanish. He didn't care about percentages and told me to be flexible and go on stage to translate for the kids so they could get an idea of what it would be like to give their testimonies in a church setting via a translator. I felt like a fool and did a lot of faking—and a disservice to the beautiful and flowery Spanish language—as I did my best at translating. I watched the doors and hoped that no one who actually spoke Spanish would walk into our training session.

Later, in Tijuana, Tom asked me to translate while he led a monolingual Spanish speaker to faith in Jesus. At first, I reminded him again that I was not fluent in Spanish, but in no uncertain terms, Tom told me to just do it. What followed surprised me and gave me a sneak peek at the supernatural power of God, which is not limited by our limitations. I was enabled to help Tom explain the Gospel, though it was beyond my Spanish-language skills, in a strange way that I couldn't fully comprehend at the time and probably will not on this side of eternity.

> *I was enabled to help Tom explain the Gospel, though it was beyond my Spanish-language skills, in a strange way that I couldn't fully comprehend at the time and probably will not on this side of eternity.*

Our youth pastor was not a cautious kind of guy. At that time, I was learning the Spanish language under the teaching of a Mexican professor, who told our class that the city of Tijuana led the world in murders per capita. He was familiar with the area and explained some of the reasons that students should not spend Easter vacation partying in the border town. He described some of the violence that goes unprosecuted. I tried to communicate this to Tom, but he was unimpressed. Our group would take walks—sometimes at night—to shop for Mexican sweet bread, candy, and things that are illegal in my hometown. Some of the boys bought switchblades, brass knuckles, and fireworks. Later, while we waited in line at the border to reenter the U.S., I was hoping our bus would not be searched because I knew there was contraband on board.

Tom was our bus driver, which was the most outrageous part of the trip. I spoke with my eldest son twenty-five years later, and he asked me if I still remembered Tom's bus driving. It was unforgettable and unbelievable. Tom liked to do everything with panache, which is just the sort of thing a youth pastor needs to keep high schoolers engaged, but it did nothing to give us confidence in his bus-driving skills. Tom would drive with an open newspaper on his lap, which he read at times when he thought the road did not need his undivided attention. It got worse when he invited the bleached-blonde babe who was his wife to sit on his lap while he was driving. When we pulled away from the Tijuana church to head homeward, I noticed the arrows on the street signs, which indicated Tom had been parking and driving us the wrong way on a one-way street around the church!

The harrowing Tijuana bus trip

If my home church had asked me to write an evaluation of the high school Great Commission trip, I would have titled the report "Chaos in Tijuana." Tom's lack of wisdom about the physical safety of his students was disconcerting, and the whole trip felt like one unsafe or goofy event after another. The students had a great time; the chaperones came home exhausted.

This second Tijuana trip had required preparation and prayer. That investment paid off and delivered an outcome that felt more purposeful than the first trip, in spite of the chaos. I do caution

Singing and puppet show for our Vacation Bible School in Tijuana

against volunteering for assignments with youth-group missions without first assessing your patience and energy reserves.

When you return from a Great Commission assignment, you have to chew up and digest your experience. Frontline assignments require immersion in a foreign culture while simultaneously engaging in productive fieldwork, which is difficult. It is especially difficult on short-term assignments because there's no time up front for assimilation. The challenge of that dual tasking is more about getting prayed up and showing up with a humble servant's heart than having any particular skill set. When God multiplied my Spanish-speaking skills that were needed for evangelism on the streets of Tijuana, it was an aha moment. It started me thinking missionally, and afterward, I wanted to go back to the field for an opportunity to *live* missionally. I just needed to ditch the teenagers and the reckless youth pastor!

The important takeaway from my second assignment in Tijuana came to me through the wisdom of my Mexican Spanish-language professor. He described the situation in Tijuana as a treacherous border town where hell is unrestrained. This is a fairly good description of the sort of places that need Great Commission workers.

My Mexican professor also mentioned that if he had a son or daughter who was planning to leave the safety of home to go into the treacherous border town of Tijuana, he would lock them in a closet. That type of thinking makes sense to most parents.

Conversely, God has different messaging for *His* sons and daughters. He commands His children to leave the safety of home to go into hellish places by the power of the Gospel until

> *God commands His children to leave the safety of home to go into hellish places by the power of the Gospel until Christians have discipled every nation, and every nation rises to its calling in Christ. This is called the Great Commission.*

Tijuana Vacation Bible School taught by our youth group

Christians have discipled every nation, and every nation rises to its calling in Christ. This is called the Great Commission.

RUMINATIONS

My two trips to Tijuana demonstrated the benefit of preparing for mission assignments. I usually spend more time preparing for trips than time spent on location, and it is well worth the effort. This is especially true of short-term work because you have to hit the ground running, with no time for assimilation. There were times when I felt like I was in over my head (and I was) because I wasn't

Our youth group with some of our Vacation Bible School students in Tijuana

prepared. God always rescued me, but it's important to do our part to prepare for ministry. If you are a team member, you don't want to weaken the team because of your failure to take your job seriously.

Having said that, I also learned that God was prepared to use me regardless of my limitations, failures, and inadequate preparation. I discovered that opportunities beyond my paygrade were plentiful just for showing up with a humble heart and a willing spirit. There were also many opportunities for doing significant tasks for the

Kingdom that were disguised as unimportant and/or unpleasant (like changing diapers).

I also began to come to terms with the treacherous nature of fieldwork, which was significant because of my predisposition to be fearful and worrisome.

1. Why is it important to adequately prepare for a mission assignment, including such things as cultivating a spirit-filled life, securing a team of prayer support, learning about the culture, and understanding the objectives of your assignment?

2. Describe something you did for God that you really didn't want to do (like chaperone a youth mission trip), but it turned out to be beneficial.

3. How has God used you in a way that was beyond your plans and limitations?

4. Why is fieldwork usually located in treacherous territory where hell has to be restrained by the power of the Gospel?

TWO

GUATEMALA AND THE BOY WHO SMILED

*Therefore I urge you, brothers and sisters, by the mercies of God,
to present your bodies [dedicating all of yourselves, set apart] as a
living sacrifice, holy and well-pleasing to God, which is your rational
(logical, intelligent) act of worship.* (Romans 12:1)

Great Commission work requires sacrifice. God wants some of us to leave the safety and comfort of home to go to the front lines, where sharing the Gospel is always going to be costly, inconvenient, or both. Sometimes mission work is physically unsafe. It has been said that the safest place to be is in the center of God's will. Of course, that is not true from a flesh-and-bones perspective. Some have become sick, injured, or even killed on the mission field. But we all live either Biblically or recklessly, and the better choice is always Biblical living, regardless of the risk.

What choice will you and I make about going to the front lines? Most of us play it safe at home and miss out on all the rewards and adventure. If missionaries were a branch of the military, they would be Marines, because the Marines are typically the ones leading the charge. The exceptionally courageous missionaries end up in far-away places like Africa, where most of us dare not go because we're not even brave enough to get all the necessary vaccines.

What could be more audacious and purposeful than frontline mission work? It is the leading edge of the Kingdom of God on earth.

I stumbled into mission work because I enjoy travel and adventure, and because I'm a bit impulsive. I would never have left home for my next short-term mission trip to Guatemala had I known what was awaiting me. My eldest son, who was thirteen years old at the time, wanted to join the team, but it was a good thing he did not because it was for mature audiences only.

There was an ongoing civil war between the Guatemalan government and leftist insurgent groups that would not officially end for another seven years after our visit in 1989. However, Guatemalans thought the winds of change were blowing. The sitting president was the first one elected under the country's new constitution in 1985. He had promised to end political violence. However, institutional terrorism persisted through death squads and disappearances, although this was camouflaged by an initial decline in violence, followed by a misinformation campaign enabled by government control of the press.

Guatemala City dump

Completely aside from the violent political landscape, our mission trip started out scary and degenerated into full-blown fear. We landed in Guatemala City, without a clue to the frightening experiences that would unfold during our trip. Everyone on the team felt the stress of our first-day excursion to the Guatemala City dump.

It was like a vision of hell. Gene and his Guatemalan wife were our leaders, and Gene decided to give us the shock treatment upfront. We all piled into a van that was too small for our group, and we headed for the Guatemala City dump. We had been briefed that the dump was a dangerous place where even the police were reluctant to go because of the violence and crime. But nothing could have prepared us for what we observed as we looked out the windows of our van.

The experience was an assault on our senses. You could smell the stench before you could see the huge piles of trash. There are no words to explain the sight of adults and children sifting through garbage for their livelihood, among pigs as well as raw sewage.

Spontaneous fires erupted here and there from the methane gas generated by the decaying heaps of garbage. The scorched earth prohibited the growth of any vegetation. Trash was strewn everywhere, with thousands of sealed plastic bags full of more garbage. Disbelief silenced everyone in the van. Then I noticed the oddest thing. A cute little boy, who was squatting in the squalor with his mother and sifting through the garbage, noticed I was taking his picture and smiled for the photo! I'll never understand his sweet smile.

The boy who smiled

We drove past the boy with our van doors locked. The dirt roads were uneven, and we pitched from one side to the other. There had been heavy rains, so in the middle of the dump, much to our horror, we became stuck in the mud! We sat there for a minute as an ominous crowd of men surrounded us. The silence was broken when one of the men in the van asked, "What are we going to do now?"

We had no option except to slide open the door of our van, get out, and push. To our surprise and relief, the crowd around us helped us to push the van out of the putrid-smelling mud, and we were on our way. God showed up at that moment in time in a way that none of us will ever forget.

At the border of the dump, there was a large, ramshackle building that was a church for the people who lived there. Painted on the side of the rustic church was Acts 16:31. God *is* present everywhere, even in the most hellish environments where people live in tiny homes made from sheets of plastic, cardboard, and other scraps pulled from heaps of rubbish.

After leaving the dump, we went to a nearby location to distribute food to hungry people who did not complain about standing in line to receive plastic bags filled with beans and rice.

"Believe in the Lord Jesus [as your personal Savior and entrust yourself to Him] and you will be saved" (Acts 16:31).

We also helped with the construction of a room addition for a widow with eight children, whose husband had been accidentally killed by the police. She and her children all slept in one room, but we helped build a room addition onto her house so she could rent it out as a source of income for her and her children.

Also, we walked around a small town and invited children to come to our vacation Bible school at a local church. At Bible school, we used "Wordless Books," which is a concept originated with Charles Spurgeon. The colors of the book pages are a catechism of the basic tenets of the Gospel, designed for cross-cultural or illiterate audiences. We made the books from felt and used them to preach the Gospel to children through an interpreter.

> *God is present everywhere, even in the most hellish environments where people live in tiny homes made from sheets of plastic, cardboard, and other scraps pulled from heaps of rubbish.*

We also spent a day offering support to a young woman named Karen. She had founded a small school on the outskirts of the dump, which also doubled as an orphanage by night for some of the students. She had driven a van all the way from the United States to Guatemala, where she began a ministry to the children who lived at the city dump.

Just as I was beginning to think I could manage all the foreign input that was flooding my senses, I noticed my arms felt itchy and dotted with what looked like chickenpox. When I signed up for the trip, I didn't know I would end up at a doctor's office in Guatemala, struggling to understand the Spanish-speaking doctor. But there I was, listening to the doctor's words with my limited Spanish skills, when he said "parasito." Afterward, my translator told me the doctor had diagnosed me with a common and contagious malady called *sarna*, which she said was insignificant and similar to lice. The doctor prescribed a bar of medicated soap for scrubbing my body and gave instructions to boil all my clothing and bed linens.

Something was lost in the translation of my diagnosis, which turned out to be wonderful. Had I known at the time that sarna was the equivalent of scabies in English, it would

> *I knew that mission work involved skin in the game, but I did not think it would be so literal, and I learned it was not a game.*

have made my situation emotionally catastrophic. It was good that I did not know there were parasites that were using my body as their host and burrowing beneath my skin to lay eggs. I knew that mission work involved skin in the game, but I did not think it would be so literal, and I learned it was not a game.

I slept with the lights on at night because I was told that the tiny parasites were more active in darkness. What looked like chicken-

pox was my body's reaction to the infestation. Parasites from pigs at the dump had hitchhiked on the bodies of children who attended Karen's school. Karen had told us that there were so many local parasites that part of her income came from selling the children's waste products to scientists who used what she sold them for research. I had stayed behind to hold down the fort while my team members took Karen out for a well-deserved meal. I would never have volunteered to do that if I had known that the result would

A little girl poses for a photograph in the countryside near Lake Atitlán.

A young mother weaves colorfully dyed thread to make fabric on her
handmade loom in the countryside of Guatemala.

be a parasite infestation that came from the pigs at the dump! The
team knew I was contagious, which required me to be set apart
from my friends in a way that I did not want to be set apart. It was
a disgusting way to end my assignment.

After we had completed our assignment, we went shopping,
which in Guatemala is noteworthy. The country is known for colorful handwoven textiles made by beautiful indigenous women on
looms out in the countryside. I tried to conceal my thrill of shopping
from the team because it felt so unspiritual. I hated to admit it, but
in the moment, shopping felt like the highlight of my trip.

Beyond the fleeting pleasure of shopping in Guatemala, there
were significant and lasting impressions from the trip that were
best appreciated in retrospect, especially the interactions with the
children at the orphanage and the little boy who lived at the dump
but still found a reason to smile.

Despite the messy, risky, and sometimes frightening nature of frontline mission work, it is without a doubt the most purposeful and adventurous life experience available to followers of Jesus. However, my ten days in Guatemala made me feel like the screaming lady in the suspension-bridge scene in *Indiana Jones and the Temple of Doom*. Since childhood, I've been inclined to panic and scream easily. Therefore, I stayed safely and comfortably at home for the next five years, hoping to grow thicker skin and watching *Indiana Jones* movies when I wanted some make-believe adventure in my life.

RUMINATIONS

Successful mission work requires sacrifice. It's easier to stay in your rut in the comfort of your home. We were warned that Guatemala could be unsafe and out of our comfort zone.

There was a lot of training and preparation for the trip, but hearing about danger or even watching it dramatized on a screen is different than experiencing it in real life. When you feel adrenalin increasing your blood flow and breathing rate to prepare you for fight or flight, you know you are out of your comfort zone. Adventure is often an uncomfortable place to be.

When we were stuck in the mud at the dump, I thought I might not make it home. We all knew the locks on our vehicle were not going to save us. It was a huge relief when God did.

Later in the trip, when I was diagnosed with a parasitic infestation, it felt like too much discomfort for a ten-day trip. When I came home, I had to boil my clothing and tell my children not to touch me.

Poverty and parasites are horrible. The comforts of home are underrated. I returned home thinking maybe Great Commission adventure was overrated. However, what mission work lacks in comfort, it makes up for in a satisfying sense of purpose.

1. Why is personal involvement in Kingdom work worthwhile, even if it requires sacrifice and discomfort?

2. How have you sacrificed something because of your faith in Christ?

3. It was sickening to watch children and adults digging through garbage for their sustenance. Why do you think a little boy digging through garbage would still be able to smile for a photo?

THREE

BELIZE JUNGLE CRUISE

Go therefore and make disciples of all the nations [help the people to learn of Me, believe in Me, and obey My words], baptizing them in the name of the Father and of the Son and of the Holy Spirit.
(Matthew 28:19)

After five years of staying safely and comfortably at home, a pastor at church set me up for my next Great Commission adventure in Belize. The pastor connected me with a church planter in Central America. N. T. Dellinger and his wife, Joy, had lived in Belize most of their adult lives. They arranged for me to teach English-language classes at a church site in Belize City. The free classes were popular and attracted unbelievers, bringing them in contact with the local church for the purpose of evangelism. I completed two assignments as an English-language teacher in Belize, once with a friend and her husband and another time with my younger son.

On the trip with my friend and her husband, I set myself up for some significant problems before leaving home. My friend volunteered to join me on the assignment. She is a singer and guitar player, which I knew would enhance English-language classes. However, her husband wanted to come along, and he was not a Christian. I was uncomfortable with including an unbeliever on the trip but failed to prevent it from happening, and there were consequences.

My friend's husband lost his passport at the border of Belize and Guatemala. He rented a car and did not use the correct credit card that would have provided rental-car insurance, so he was forced to pay for a costly collision with a hit-and-run driver. The tire on his rental car blew out on a road far away from services. He disliked all the insects, and he was a mosquito magnet. There was no air conditioning, and he hated the hot, humid weather. He disliked the dogs that barked at night and the early-morning food vendor who blew a shrill and annoying whistle to announce his presence in the neighborhood.

The three of us used our weekends off to visit one of the nearby islands off the coast of Belize, where we went on the snorkel trip from hell. While we were out in deep water, my friend's husband developed leg cramps and a mask leak, so he grabbed his wife, creating fear that they were both going to drown.

In another incident out on the island, the man was bitten by a dog. It was convenient that he was a physician, because he had brought medical supplies. The day my friend's husband was attacked by the dog, we had chosen separate activities, and I had my own remarkable incident. I had a run-in with a car while riding a resort bicycle. I was wearing flip-flops and was dressed appropriately for the hot, tropical climate, and there were no helmets available. I had jumped on the bicycle, propelling it downhill to get off to a quick start, but learned too late that the bicycle chain was off the sprockets. Because the chain was off the sprockets, the bicycle quickly accelerated, I could not brake, and I had limited control of the steering. Unfortunately, I was moving fast and headed toward a car on the dirt road adjacent to the resort, on a course to T-bone the car on the driver's side. Then suddenly, what should have happened did not happen. I can't explain in human terms what did happen, but some sort of collision occurred, the car passed, and yet, I found myself upright and straddling the bicycle with only a minor scratch on my leg. In an instant, I went from being horrified with the anticipation of an inevitable and significant collision of metal and flesh to being very surprised, safe, and sound, as the dust from the unpaved road settled. The driver of the car had not slowed down but had continued straight ahead for quite a while after we collided, but then he returned to the scene, looking astonished. I was visibly shaken and not exactly sure why I was not injured. God had done some sort of intervention to save me from what should have been much more than a scratch on my leg. I didn't feel the impact of the car, only the slow-motion perception of the end of my right handlebar softly touching the driver's window. I think the scratch on my leg was meant to confirm that the accident really happened. The incident didn't feel like ordinary life because it was extraordinary life. When I reunited with my friends, they told me about the dog attack, and I told them about my bicycle accident that should have been a calamity but was instead a miraculous and merciful intervention by God.

Things only calmed down after my friend and her husband left early because of the imminent birth of their first grandchild. After my friend returned from the assignment, she wrote a letter of appreciation to her prayer supporters, which included the repeated phrase, "It could have been worse." In the letter, she listed the many problems her husband had experienced, as well as the outcomes. Those outcomes truly could have been worse, especially regarding the dog bite. The man's son was also a physician, and he advised his father

N. T. with my friend and her husband, who had the worst trip of his life!

to be treated for rabies, but the man refused. He never developed symptoms of rabies, but it caused us concern for several weeks after the trip. My friend closed the letter to her prayer team with her husband's final evaluation of his time in Belize. He told her it was the worst trip of his life. I learned the hard way that bringing unbelievers on mission trips invites complications that can compromise the mission and negatively impact everyone on the team.

English-language students in Belize

After my friend and her husband left Belize, my assignment was to house-sit N. T. and Joy Dellinger's home by myself. Some of the seminary students were living on the property, and it was my job to feed them dinner. It was a little scary to be alone at night in the house. The Dellingers had fortified the place after numerous break-ins, but when the electricity failed one night, everything was eerily dark. I was on the computer at the time, and I was surprised that the computer was unaffected by the blackout. I emailed my eldest son about what I thought was a miracle, but he responded to my message by explaining that the computer undoubtedly had an uninterruptable power supply, which people use in countries with undependable power sources. He was correct.

Despite all the drama of including an unbeliever on the trip and the inconvenient power outages, the Belize assignment opened my eyes to what the Great Commission is supposed to look like. It was in Belize that I had the once-in-a-lifetime privilege of serving alongside two giants in the faith. N. T. and Joy were deeply committed to the Great Commission and pushed forward God's agenda, regardless of what it cost them personally.

In 1964, the Dellingers left the "good life" behind to become career missionaries living an Indiana Jones lifestyle, especially at the startup of their ministry. They packed all their belongings into a Jeep and drove from Tucson, Arizona, to Belize. When they arrived, the country was called British Honduras, but it was beginning its transition from being the last British colony on the mainland of America to being a self-governing country. It would be renamed Belize in 1973 and gain full independence in 1981. Because it was previously a British colony, the official language of Belize is English, although a variety of languages is spoken in the country. N. T. and Joy became fluent Spanish speakers to facilitate their ministry to those who spoke Spanish.

The Dellingers' first residence in Belize was small and had no electricity and no running water, but they were especially fond of their first home on the mission field. N. T. began preaching in an established church, while also discipling young men to ready them for church planting throughout Belize and other surrounding countries in the Northern Triangle. Joy taught a girls' club and Sunday School. She also founded a school for forty-five children, teaching the equivalent of grades one through eight in a one-room schoolhouse.

Today, more than half of Belize is subtropical jungle and rainforest, but when N. T. and Joy arrived in 1964, there was more jungle and rainforest and far less infrastructure. The Dellingers took lots of boat trips on the meandering rivers, which cut paths through the jungle and were once navigated by ancient Mayans. Belize is a small country about the size of Massachusetts, with thirty-five rivers, some of which served to connect communities before paved roads and bridges were constructed. In their first year, the Dellingers were joined by a team of six college students from Michigan for a short-term Bible-school project in a place called Crooked Tree, which is an inland river island that could only be reached via an eight-hour boat journey. One can only imagine the two newly married college graduates with their first missionary team in that boat, passing crocodiles, toucans, and jaguars along the riverbanks. The team arrived unscathed at their remote destination and were grateful

> *One can only imagine the two newly married college graduates with their first missionary team in that boat, passing crocodiles, toucans, and jaguars along the riverbanks.*

for the simple sleeping accommodations that sheltered them in the jungle, which was teeming with living creatures, like the loud howler monkeys that startled them from their slumber every morning at 4 a.m. Joy described how their group learned to graciously receive food that was a sacrifice for their hosts in Crooked Tree, when an excessively underweight chicken was killed and cooked for their dinner. Their jungle adventures should have been shared with the world. The Dellingers sheltered in some odd places, and I loved hearing about an overnight stay in an abandoned vehicle in the wild terrain of Belize!

The Dellingers established churches throughout Belize, El Salvador, Guatemala, and Honduras. In addition to planting churches, N. T. and Joy had a small classroom/residence on their property to provide seminary training for pastors of their church plants. They also provided meals for the students. N. T. had earned a master's degree in theology from the Talbot School of Theology, which he put to good use as the professor to his seminary students.

The Dellingers were funded by supporters through a mission organization. During the later years of their ministry, Joy also worked long stints at the American Embassy and USAID to augment their income and increase their ability to help others.

Their Great Commission assignment included many remarkable acts of hospitality and compassion, but their outreach to refugees who had fled the civil war in El Salvador and Guatemala was exceptional. At one time, their small compound was overflowing with more than fifty people who were escaping the upheaval of the civil

N. T. and Joy Dellinger

wars. Every day, there were lines out the front door as hungry people waited for meals. It must have been exhausting to shelter, feed, and help their guests to become self-sufficient so they could move on and make room for newly displaced refugees. Of course, all the refugees were given a healthy dose of the Gospel, and N. T. seized the opportunity to disciple several of the refugees to return to their countries for the purpose of planting churches. Oscar de la Cruz was one of the refugees who returned to Guatemala to start more than thirty congregations!

I stayed in the Belize City home of the Dellingers on two occasions. Their home was infested with tropical insects, especially active after dark. I emailed my family about a recurring nightmare about cockroaches nesting in my hair. Then, one night, I woke up and there was really a cockroach in my hair! I managed to refrain from screaming out of consideration for the Dellingers. However, I beat myself on the head for the purpose of extracting the cockroach from my hair until I noticed the poor thing on the floor upside down, with legs flailing in the air. I had told Joy Dellinger that I could not bear to kill living creatures, not even cockroaches, even though she had explained the necessity of doing so for the purpose of decreasing

N. T. and Joy with my son

their exponential breeding outcomes. I decided to step on that half-beaten-to-death cockroach and have since changed my attitude about killing them.

The next morning, N. T. wanted to know why I was sleeping in the living room on the couch instead of in my bedroom. I was embarrassed as I told him about my meltdown during the night. What I didn't tell him was that I wanted to go home right then because of the cockroach incident. After all the Dellingers had tolerated for the advancement of the Kingdom of God, there I was, reacting to a cockroach like the crazed lady on the suspension bridge.

The cockroach fiasco was not my only run-in with critters in Belize. On another assignment at the Dellinger home, my son and I slept downstairs below their stilted house. The ceiling above our sleeping dorm was loaded with woodlice, which are tiny crustaceans with a segmented body and seven pairs of legs. We never saw them, but we knew they were there because of the dull white glitter-size droppings that fell from the ceiling onto everything below. Before I left for home, I noticed there were droppings in my open suitcase, so I started removing the contents so I could shake out the unwanted waste product and repack. When I removed the last few items, I was terrified by a small hopping mouse that suddenly leaped out of my suitcase. I had seen the furry little mice hopping along the roadsides, but I reacted more urgently to the one at the bottom of my suitcase. Even so, there is something about surprise wildlife encounters that add to the adventure of Great Commission work, just because you lived to talk about it.

The Dellingers were undeterred by the critters and inconveniences of Belize. They loved the people and the country, and N. T. wanted to die there with his flip-flops on and his Bible open. It was a sad day when cancer forced him to return to the U.S. for medical treatment. They were, and continue to be, an inspiration to me. Their lives were like something out of the Hebrews 11 Faith Hall of Fame for their courage and determination to be the Gospel to the people of Central America. They accomplished great things in the name of Jesus through their love, goodness, and humility, which earned them the respect even of those outside of the Christian faith.

I found that out one day when my tour guide offered me a ride home to my doorstep after a day touring the country. He had filled my ear with all sorts of negative talk about organized religion when I tried to share my faith. As we neared the home of the Dellingers, I gave the tour guide a nice tip, but when he saw where I was staying, his face fell and he asked, "You're staying with the church father?" He handed back the tip and insisted that it be donated to the Dellingers' ministry.

Not too many people would leave behind everything that wouldn't fit into a Jeep and then drive to Central America, to travel up the river to a mosquito-infested place called Crooked Tree in the middle of a subtropical rainforest. Bugs could not stop them and neither could bullets. I loved N. T.'s story about when he was on a bicycle in San Pedro Sula, Honduras, and someone held a gun to his head. He pushed the assailant's hand away and told him that he couldn't shoot him because he was a Christian. That's when the gun went off too close to his ear because the shooter's finger was on the trigger. N. T. was deaf in that ear for the rest of his life, but the man with the gun disappeared, knowing that N. T. was not going to be stopped by gunfire or anything else.

The Dellingers knew beforehand about many of the challenges and dangers they would face in Belize, from tropical diseases to killer hurricanes. But they did not know that they would be robbed by people that they were trying to help. Nor did they dream that N. T. would fall down a well and live to talk about it. N. T. probably never thought he would have a loaded gun held to his head. Nor did they anticipate that Joy would become nearly blind because of poor medical care. Undoubtedly, the biggest heartbreak was when Joy's beloved sister was murdered by a husband that they knew was a bad character, and the man was never convicted of the crime. There were so many reasons for them to pack up their bags and go home. Nevertheless, they devoted themselves to living out the Great Commission in an inspiring and exemplary way, all while having the adventure of a lifetime.

The Dellingers had hoped to write a book about their extraordinary adventures, but it never went to press. It was my great privilege to know the Dellingers and to offer this abbreviated version of their monumental life work. Far more important is the happily-ever-after ending to their story, which is that after fifty years of heroically spending every last bit of energy they had on the Great Commission, they will find their home in heaven, where they will hear their Lord tell them, "Well done, good and faithful servant" (Matthew 25:21)!

> *After fifty years of heroically spending every last bit of energy they had on the Great Commission, they will find their home in heaven, where they will hear their Lord tell them, "Well done, good and faithful servant."*

RUMINATIONS

We experienced some frightening events in Belize. It was scary riding downhill alone on a bicycle without working brakes, especially when it became apparent that I was going to crash into a car. Afterward, I was still shaking when I noticed my ministry partner and her husband walking briskly toward me to say that they had just been attacked by a dog. It was too disturbing and coincidental to process, and I still haven't figured out what it meant, but I can say that Great Commission work is not for the fainthearted!

Also in Belize, I survived a cockroach nesting in my hair, a mouse hopping out of my suitcase, and other critters in the Dellinger home, which screamed for an exterminator.

But strangely enough, Belize was one of my most treasured Great Commission experiences, primarily because of the sheer blessing of working with N. T. and Joy Dellinger. There was something richly rewarding about doing ministry alongside godly people who could not give away enough of themselves to serve the Lord in a humble and honorable way.

Joy and N. T. understood how to effectively implement the Great Commission, and I was privileged to watch them in action. Working with them was one of the great honors of my life.

1. Why is it valuable to spend time with godly people who are willing to teach and model Biblical concepts like the Great Commission?

2. Who discipled you in the faith, and what was the outcome? If you've never been discipled, are you interested in learning from others who know more than you do about Biblical living?

3. Why is it best to exclude people from mission teams who are not devout Christians?

The Dellingers

FOUR

The Pain of Poverty in El Salvador

Blessed [spiritually prosperous, happy, to be admired] are the poor in spirit [those devoid of spiritual arrogance, those who regard themselves as insignificant], for theirs is the kingdom of heaven [both now and forever]. (Matthew 5:3)

In the summer of 1995, N. T. Dellinger sent me and my six-teen-year-old daughter on an assignment to Chalchuapa, El Salvador. Once again, our Great Commission assignment was to teach English-language classes at a church site for the purpose of attracting and evangelizing outsiders. I was delighted to have my daughter as my partner because she had an interest in full-time, frontline missions and needed some real-life experience.

There was a strong connection between the Chalchuapa church and the Dellingers. The church was pastored by a father and son. The son had fled El Salvador years earlier as a draft dodger after being summoned to fight in the civil war. He was one of the refugees the Dellingers had sheltered and fed. At the Dellinger home, he had met a woman that helped cook for the refugees; she would later become his wife. After they married, they moved to the refugee's hometown in Chalchuapa, El Salvador, as church planters. He and his father were the pastors of the small church where we taught English-language classes.

When N. T. picked us up at the airport in the capital, he introduced us to our taxi driver and told us that he had just guided the driver in prayer to follow Jesus. It was a motivational start to our mission.

El Salvador was a difficult place to be sent to, partly because only three years had passed since the end of more than twelve years of a brutal civil war. We arrived and drove past the only tall building in the capital,

> *We arrived and drove past the only tall building in the capital, which had been blown apart at the top and remained untouched as a grim reminder of the war.*

which had been blown apart at the top and remained untouched as a grim reminder of the war. As we drove from the airport in the capital to Chalchuapa, it looked like the country was under the scourge of poverty.

Upon our arrival, we had a welcome dinner in the home of the younger pastor, which had no indoor plumbing. There was a pit toilet in the backyard, with a five-foot enclosure around it. There were no phones in the home. If you wanted to phone home, you had to go to a small building in town, where you paid by the minute to make a call with a poor connection. We gave up on the poor-quality calls and sent faxes to communicate with our family.

We had been told in advance that our accommodations were so nice that they called the place "the Palace." It was located across the street from a police station, which added a layer of security. Unfortunately, the church had been booted out of "the Palace" just prior to our arrival. The church had moved to the compound where we ended up staying, which might have been called "the Prison."

The gated and barred church compound was also the residence of the older pastor and his wife, as well as their daughter and their daughter's five-year-old child. They all slept in one of the bedrooms to temporarily give me and my daughter the only other bedroom

My daughter and little Whitney

on-site. We loved the five-year-old girl, whose name was Whitney. She brightened our days with her huge, dark eyes and Shirley Temple curls. Whitney was our little companion during the day while her mother worked at a local leather business. You could tell the grandparents loved the child, but they were sad about the circumstances of her birth. We developed a friendship with Whitney's mother and were taken aback when we were offered the opportunity to adopt the child. That didn't happen, but the child was a treasure, and her cherubic smile is in a framed portrait photo that still hangs on a wall in my home.

Our assignment in El Salvador was humbling because nothing prepares the average American to dwell among the average Salvadoran so soon after the end of a civil war. We had previously interacted with the poor, but we had never lived among them. In addition to the lack of creature comforts, the language barrier made us feel isolated. We tried to focus on our assignment of attracting outliers into the church with our offering of English-language classes, but we were the most obvious outliers.

The younger pastor's wife spoke English and would sometimes take us on walking tours of the town and fill us in on what was going on around us. She briefly showed up every day to bring us our only substantial meal of the day. She did not bring food for the older pastor and his wife, but they secretly ate every scrap of our leftovers when we were out of sight.

The church compound had a simple outdoor kitchen with a butane camping stove and a large cement sink that drained into a pail, but no refrigerator. Our host placed a bucket of water in our room because the landlord turned off the water from late afternoon until the next morning. My daughter pointed to our water reserve and said, "Look, Mom, the water in the bucket is jiggling!" I thought she was being silly, but she was not. There must have been some sort of amoeba-type creatures in the water.

Our no-nonsense bedroom

Our kitchen, completely open to the elements on one side

El Salvador was an especially tough assignment for my daughter because she became sick with intestinal problems, as well as a significant skin allergy. During the first few days of our assignment, I remember her saying to me, "Mom, do you realize we've only been here for three days?" It was a very long month.

The church compound had only one bathroom for us and the four residents that lived there permanently. We should have been grateful for an indoor toilet that flushed, but the bathroom was indescribably horrible. The worst part was the enormous black spider that lived in the bathroom. We kept one another updated on its ever-changing location. Since then, it has been my habit to take sticky spider traps on mission trips. Visitors to the United States from developing countries must think our bathrooms are shrines designed for a religious experience.

The bathroom situation in Chalchuapa was only made worse by the adjacent room with a shower. I am about to divulge a secret that has been concealed for many years. My daughter and I hated the shower facility so intensely that we decided not to shower the entire workweek, even in that hot and humid climate. We spent the weekends nine miles away in the town of Santa Ana, where we showered and watched English-speaking television and stuffed ourselves on delicious Salvadoran food.

Little did I know what peril I was inviting because of our weekend escapes to Santa Ana, which was near the capital. I knew when we left the United States that El Salvador was on the State Department's "Do Not Travel" list. What I did not know was that for years before, during, and after the civil war, El Salvador has been one of the most dangerous countries on earth, and the capital is the most dangerous part of the country. In 2015, it earned the title of murder capital of the world. We would have been safer if we had not taken public transportation on weekends to our hotel, which did not have room service. I can pass for Latina, but my daughter's appearance gave away her identity as a gringo, so she stayed in the room while I went out alone to buy food. One time, I became lost and walked around for about thirty minutes before I found my way back to the hotel. I wondered why there were security guards with big rifles guarding the banks, hotels, and some of the businesses. I'm thankful that God protects idiots!

My daughter and I should have stayed in Chalchuapa. We were told that the town was so far out on the frontier of the country near the border of Guatemala that its inhabitants barely felt the effects of the civil war. However, the curbs of several of the street corners had been painted with the letters FMLN, which were the territorial markings of the leftist opposition group during the civil war. Before fleeing the country years earlier, the younger pastor of the church had been ordered off a bus in Chalchuapa before it was set ablaze by a leftist group.

The town of Chalchuapa was the place I first learned that cockroaches can fly. I went to the post office to mail a postcard and found out that the postage stamps had various pictures of colorful insects, which seemed completely appropriate for a place that had no lack of bugs. I was unaware at the time of the many venomous scorpions, centipedes, and spiders in the country, or I probably would have been less concerned about cucarachas.

Looking back, the town of Chalchuapa was a unique place to visit. I've never met anyone who has been there—even among the Salvadorans I have met in the United States. In 1995, it was a charming town where time appeared to have stood still. The town had impressive potential as a travel destination. There were narrow cobblestone streets that were put into place before anyone thought about two-way automobile traffic. Chalchuapa is home to several archeological sites that are not well known to tourists, including Tazumal, which is a significant pre-Columbian Mayan pyramid. There is also a beautiful old colonial-style Catholic church in Chalchuapa, and a large and creepy pond called Cuzcachapa Lagoon, with local folklore that has attempted to explain its ghostly appearance. The lagoon would be a great location to film a sci-fi thriller.

The food alone was worth the trip. It was fascinating to watch the women on the street corners grilling pupusas. They began with a ball of masa, and the finished product was a delicious, thick corn tortilla stuffed with beans, cheese, or other fillings and topped with shredded vegetables.

Another highlight of the trip was our Salvadoran students. Prior to the assignment, Joy Dellinger had prepared me via phone to teach the unjaded and respectful students. They were humble and welcoming. Most of them spoke no English at all. They treated us like celebrities—especially my shy and pretty blonde daughter, who was a bit overwhelmed with all the attention. The students were highly motivated, cooperative, and appreciative of our time and attention. The pastors of the church would show up at class unannounced and speak to the students at length about the Christian faith, and our students listened attentively.

The church service was also something special that I had never experienced. By comparison, my church format at home seemed like a performance. These church members had very little wealth, but perhaps that was the source of the beauty of their worship. At first, I was uncomfortable with parts of the worship services. There were times when everyone stood and prayed individually out loud at the same time, which was initially disconcerting. I was confused about what was happening, so I looked around like a kindergartner on the first day of school searching for clues about what was expected of me. That's when I realized that the praying worshippers were unaware of anyone else in the room. After I moved beyond my attention-deficit-brain's reaction to so many individuals enthusiastically praying out loud at the same time in a foreign language, the worship became less foreign and more beautiful to me.

The church service had no gifted musicians, no talented singers, no polished sermons, no fancy sanctuary, and no well-dressed worshippers. There was also no apparent spiritual arrogance or any sense of prideful significance. There was an inexplicable loveliness about the way they worshipped Jesus so simply and authentically. Perhaps this sort of joyful and participatory worship only happens among the poor, where people are aware of their dependence upon God for their daily bread and feel blessed by something as simple as the provision of food.

Near the end of our very long month in Chalchuapa, I looked for my passport but could not find it. I had left it at the local bank, and prior to our departure, a bank employee returned it to the younger pastor of our church. Years later, I reminded my adult daughter about my lost passport because she had told me at the time that she intended to leave as originally planned, with or without me. I jokingly suggested that perhaps she was not serious about leaving me behind, but she was serious.

My daughter did not become a career missionary. She did not know ahead of time that our accommodations would be beyond spartan and that she would become sick. She may not have gone if she had known what awaited her in El Salvador. But if she had said no to the assignment, she would have only vague memories of a nondescript birthday month in August of 1995 and a wasted opportunity of eternal proportions.

> *Poverty hit us the hardest. You can't fully understand poverty until you sit in the middle of it.*

RUMINATIONS

It was good to have my daughter along as my teaching partner for English-language classes in El Salvador. We enjoyed our gracious hosts, the sweet and humble students, and the church members that worshipped every Sunday at the compound where we lived and taught classes.

El Salvador was one of my most difficult mission trips, with many challenges that made our month-long commitment seem like a very long time. My daughter's illness, staying locked inside the gated and barred compound, losing my passport, and the language barrier were discouraging.

Poverty hit us the hardest. You can't fully understand poverty until you sit in the middle of it. The compound didn't include a house—only three separate structures: a partly open rectangular shelter used for worship, another structure with two bedrooms, and the dreadful latrine with a shower. The landlord would shut off our water supply late in the day, and we had to wait for him to turn it back on in the morning. The limited water supply sometimes created obvious problems with the toilet and shower. You had to go outdoors to get to the bathroom, which was a challenge during the torrential downpours that made you wonder about the integrity of the roof. Most of the people didn't have cars, telephones, or toilets that flushed.

Poverty is miserable, and by the end of the month, we had allowed it to wear us down. There are probably many missionaries who live in poverty, but I have never personally met any of them. Those who endure poverty long-term have my respect and admiration.

We returned home exhausted and kissed the ground of our motherland.

1. Why is living in extreme poverty in a developing nation difficult to endure for Americans?

2. How long do you think you would be able to survive below the poverty level in a foreign country?

3. What are the emotional effects of a language barrier?

FIVE

ORPHANAGE EMMANUEL REUNION

Your own soul is nourished when you are kind. (Proverbs 11:17 TLB)

The next country I checked off my bucket list was Honduras. I wanted to visit all the countries in Central America and then move on to South America. However, that desire began to fade, and I started to think about dropping anchor in Honduras.

I joined a church team of fifty youth and adults on an assignment at a large orphanage near the capital of Honduras. I was the kitchen manager, planning and preparing meals for our team and the orphanage staff.

I volunteered several times at the orphanage with a youth pastor named Andrae. He is my all-time favorite youth leader, as well as my bigger-than-life friend. Andrae is a great chef and demonstrates his love for others by fixing them delicious food. It was a bit annoying at first when Andrae wanted me to prepare labor-intensive meals, especially since we were in a remote location without a local source for buying groceries. We had one chance to purchase everything we needed at a large grocery warehouse before we headed to the orphanage. Perhaps Andrae thought that simple meals weren't good enough for the hard-working skeleton staff at the orphanage. The staff appreciated our extra efforts, which included theme dinners with decorations and an international menu.

I loved being in the kitchen and received a lot of support from Andrae, who also supplied me with kitchen volunteers. He knew how to cook for crowds and helped me calculate the amount of food to prepare for our big group. He took the lead whenever we fed the entire orphanage as well as our team and the orphanage staff, which meant feeding almost five hundred people! We cooked animals raised and dressed on-site at the orphanage farm. Once we made fried chicken for everyone. Another time, he buried and slow-cooked a large pig, Hawaiian style!

Roasting a pig Hawaiian style to feed everyone

We just happened to be on assignment every year for the birthday of the woman who founded the orphanage with her husband.

Lydia and David with the freshly baked birthday cake

So, we baked and decorated a huge specialty cake to honor the beloved Mama Lydia and also provided a birthday-theme dinner.

In 1989, David and Lydia Martinez founded Orphanage Emmanuel. They began with a handful of children on a thousand acres in a Caribbean pine forest, without the benefit of electricity or running water. The orphanage has the unique ministry of sheltering hundreds of street children. The orphanage population had grown to five hundred children the last time I checked their website. The policy of the founders is that they don't turn away anyone that they are capable of sheltering, because no child should have to live on the streets. The children live in cabins with older teens assigned to each dwelling to supervise the younger children. It's

not the best situation in terms of adult-to-child ratios, but it is a practical way to shelter street kids who would otherwise be hungry, homeless, and at the mercy of street gangs and human traffickers.

The children attend a Christian school located

The feeding of the five hundred

on the orphanage property. Daily devotions in the early mornings and church on Sundays are mandatory. Every child at Emmanuel receives a healthy dose of the Gospel on a daily basis. The founders are aware that the shortage of adults for discipling the children makes their dream of raising up godly Honduran citizens difficult, but it is their core objective.

David and Lydia had to overcome many obstacles to establish the large orphanage, including corruption and opposition from the local police. They gave up their fancy cars and their life of ease in the United States because of a Great Commission calling to help hundreds of street children. They sold everything they owned in the United States and used the money to buy the orphanage property, which they thought was ten acres but turned out to be 970 acres! They never had their own biological children, but they've parented thousands of children who provide them with nourishment for their souls in exchange for their outreach to the boys and girls.

Orphanage Emmanuel is understaffed, and they welcome workers to help care for the children and also to complete special projects. If you are interested in finding out more about the orphanage, please visit them on Facebook.

The life stories of the children at the orphanage were almost unbelievable. We could not comprehend how it was possible that underage children were allowed to live on the streets. We wondered why there was not a government safety net to provide for the basic needs of the boys and girls. David and Lydia saw the screaming need and did something about it in the way described in James 1:27. They have made it their life work to provide the basics

> *We could not comprehend how it was possible that underage children were allowed to live on the streets. We wondered why there was not a government safety net to provide for the basic needs of the boys and girls.*

of food, shelter, education, and spiritual training for children who would otherwise have no hope. We were awed by the great provision that David and Lydia had made for so many children. One evening after dinner, we arranged for a solemn time of foot washing for the couple, with the students kneeling to demonstrate appreciation for so much goodness and sacrifice in the name of Jesus.

We saw some of the sad consequences for children who do not have parents to provide them with basic medical care. The first year we went to the orphanage, we noticed that many of the children had a contagious skin disease called impetigo. Fortunately, Dr. Robert Meyer went there the following year with the medical expertise and medicine to resolve that problem. There was an infirmary on-site that provided basic first-aid services and helped the children with health issues like contagious boils, conjunctivitis, botfly infestations, and lice.

We had to come to terms with the varmint population at the orphanage, which was crawling with nocturnal cockroaches, rats, fire ants, huge black moths that looked like bats on the walls, hideous gigantic grasshoppers, enormous frogs that sounded like sheep bleating at night, swarms of flies and wasps, tarantulas, scorpions, and venomous snakes. Worst of all were the dreaded botflies! They are nightmarish creatures you can google if you have an interest in the worst and most disgusting parasite in Central America.

In between my kitchen responsibilities and dodging disease and pestilence, I walked around the large campus to visit with the children. That's when I found out that being the kitchen manager was not the main reason I was sent to the orphanage that year. I noticed a six-year-old girl who was crying alone. What could be sadder than a little orphan girl crying alone? I loved little Angelina the minute I met her. She appeared to be inconsolable. My Spanish skills are limited, and Angelina was difficult to understand because of her sobbing. With God enhancing my Spanish-speaking skills, I was able to comprehend that the little girl was a new arrival at the large, understaffed orphanage. She had two younger brothers, from whom she had been separated because the children are placed in dwellings by gender and age. All she wanted was to be with her little brothers, but she didn't know where to find them. I believe God brought me there that year to answer the prayers of a broken little girl who desper-

> *I believe God brought me there that year to answer the prayers of a broken little girl who desperately needed to be with the only portion of her family that had not been forever lost.*

ately needed to be with the only portion of her family that had not been forever lost. None of the overworked staff had time to notice Angelina's cry for help and simply walk her by the hand over to her brothers for a hug. That was my job. It filled my heart with purpose to be there at that moment in time when three little hearts became united and filled with exceeding joy.

Anyone with the time would have done what I did for Angelina and her brothers, but it is rare (if you stay at home) to find such rich opportunities for the kindness that nourishes the soul described in the Living Bible paraphrase of Proverbs 11:17. Great Commission work with orphans is loaded with the perfect setup for giving to others who have nothing to give in return. My experience with Angelina and her little brothers was indescribably rewarding. Every

Angelina reunited with her younger brothers

time I returned to Orphanage Emmanuel, it became less and less important for me to move on to Panama, Nicaragua, and Costa Rica. I never did visit the remainder of the Central American countries on my bucket list, because the Great Commission became more meaningful than my travel plans.

RUMINATIONS

My five trips to Orphanage Emmanuel were almost too enjoyable to be Great Commission work. I loved being on Andrae's mission team because he knew how to mix hard work with fun.

Switching from English-language teacher to kitchen manager at the orphanage was a pleasant change. Spoiling the orphans, staff, and mission team with tasty meals was fun. It was especially wonderful when we made the decorated and made-from-scratch carrot cake for Mama Lydia's birthday celebrations during our visits.

Another reason that my time at Orphanage Emmanuel was so enjoyable was the meaningful opportunity that God gave me to help Angelina find her younger brothers. It was a purposeful experience that was soul nourishing.

I eventually moved on to another ministry and felt so missed when one of Andrae's team members told me that she wanted me to come back because the team had to make their own peanut butter and jelly sandwiches when I wasn't there in the kitchen to prepare tastier lunches. This same team member and I had shared an embarassing moment together at the orphanage when she came into the communal bathroom and complained about something I had done, not knowing that I was in the bathroom stall and could hear every word she was saying. Her remark was insignificant, and I felt more embarrassed for her than offended by her. I was too cowardly to confront her about the matter, so I stayed in the bathroom stall for a long time until I was sure she was gone. Later, I joked with Andrae about the humorous situation and the mild comment the girl had made when she didn't know I was listening. I didn't want Andrae to mention the incident to the student. However, the girl later came to me on her knees and begged me to forgive her. Andrae was serious about team unity and made sure that everyone was super respectful and considerate, especially toward the adults on the team.

1. Why is mission-team unity critically important?

2. What would it involve for you to leave everything behind and become a full-time missionary like David and Lydia? Have you prayerfully considered this option?

3. Have you ever done an act of kindness that nourished your soul?

SIX

Miracles Are Not Always Pretty

One of the synagogue officials named Jairus came up; and seeing Him, fell at His feet and begged anxiously with Him, saying, "My little daughter is at the point of death; [please] come and lay Your hands on her, so that she will be healed and live." (Mark 5:22–23)

After my son and I completed our assignment on the mainland at Orphanage Emmanuel, we flew on a prop-engine airplane to the nearby Caribbean island of Roatán. As we flew in the small plane, I began to process the events of our short-term mission trip. I was relieved that the hard work in the hot kitchen was finished, and I was ready for rest and recuperation. I didn't realize that the wildest adventure of my life was about to unfold, something that I would never believe unless I saw it with my own eyes.

I had heard that Roatán, Honduras, was the cheapest place in the world to become scuba certified, which was an irresistible hook for a frugal person who always wanted to learn to dive. My twenty-three-year-old son and I signed up for scuba certification. I had to overcome some personal fears in order to complete the open-water certification. We also explored the island, visiting an iguana reserve and escaping mad dogs that chased us on our small rented scooter.

One night, we had a dinner out on the town that can only be described as supernatural. A miracle happened, but one that I am reluctant to describe because it was messy. It was not only untidy—the whole thing was so entirely unbelievable that I'm glad my son was there with me as a witness. God orchestrated the entire event from

After our assignment on the mainland, we flew to Roatán for scuba certification.

start to finish like an intricate symphony that hung on a few critical notes for the unexpected but exhilarating finale.

My son and I were staying in the small beach town of West Bay. The white-sand beach and offshore snorkeling were breathtaking, but the best restaurants were in another nearby town. Our favorite open-air beachfront restaurant was located in West End. We traveled to West End by boat, or water taxi, as they are commonly called on the island. We left the Infinity Bay dock and were off to our destination, until the driver did a sudden U-turn and returned to the dock to pick up a couple that was hailing him.

We didn't mind since we knew the couple from our resort. In fact, they were staying in the other half of our duplex bungalow. We didn't know that God had arranged for Bob and Gloria to be our neighbors. Looking back, I marvel at the way God arranged the intersection of our lives for an unforgettable moment in time.

Our scooter. The gas station was a shed with gas in mayonnaise jars.

The couple was also going to West End for dinner, but they were planning to go to a different restaurant. After the pleasant water-taxi ride, we said farewell and parted company. However, Bob and Gloria's restaurant of choice was closed, so they walked the short distance on the white-sand streets to find us at our favorite restaurant and asked if they could join us. None of us saw what was coming, so we just carried on with the great food and conversation at the Arco de Iris Argentinian Grill. The weather and the setting were perfect, with a lovely

The duplex cabana we shared with our neighbors

view of Half Moon Bay. The sunset took our breath away, and it was as if we had been transported to a faraway world of tranquility.

While we were all enjoying the serenity and beauty of the moment, our world suddenly exploded. Gloria and I were chatting while Bob and my son were involved in a separate conversation about their diving adventures. Gloria suddenly stopped talking and looked toward her husband. She appeared to have trouble speaking. She

Water taxis waiting near the dock to give rides to West End for shopping and dining

put down her beer bottle and said, "Bob, I think I'm gonna pass out." She more than passed out. Her eyes rolled up into her head, she went limp, stopped breathing, and needed immediate CPR. Soon afterward, she exhibited agonal breathing, which is a brainstem reflex—the body's last-ditch effort to deliver oxygen to the vital organs. This condition usually precedes death. We were all terrified. I was screaming for help from anyone in the restaurant with a medical background. No one came forward to help. We helplessly watched Gloria in horror and were at a loss for what to do. When Gloria did not come back to us, I did something that was more reflexive than thoughtful action. I put my hands on her and began praying for God to revive

> *When Gloria did not come back to us, I did something that was more reflexive than thoughtful action. I put my hands on her and began praying for God to revive her in the name of Jesus.*

her in the name of Jesus. Then an amazing thing happened. Gloria came back to us in a jolt, causing the contents of her stomach and intestines to erupt from both ends. It was both shocking and thrilling to see her regain consciousness, but it did not smell good. As all eyes were on Gloria, the outcome of her return to consciousness destroyed the ambiance of the beachfront restaurant, and the owners wanted us to vacate the premises ASAP.

Gloria was embarrassed and appeared to be air hugging the vomit on the table in front of her, somehow hoping no one would see it. They brought us towels to cover up her backside and started cleaning up the mess. They couldn't find a taxi driver fast enough to remove her from the restaurant. She insisted on going back to her bungalow to change her clothes and clean up before going to the public hospital. The doctor at the hospital had no clear explanation for what had happened to her or why she suddenly came back to life without noticeable side effects. The hospital did not have sophisticated diagnostic equipment beyond an X-ray machine, but she looked good to us.

No one, including myself, would have chosen me to be sitting across the table from Gloria to prayerfully lay hands on her. God uses the most unlikely candidates to do His will, even when they are on rest and recuperation. He put me in the right place at the right time with the right person to be used in an odd and unsanitary but supernatural way. Roatán is a small island, and God probably had to scrape the bottom of the barrel to find someone who would do the job. I was unprepared and had no prior experience, nor did I ever imagine anything like this event would ever happen to me. At that time, it was the most unforgettable and purposeful moment of my life.

RUMINATIONS

The miracle at the restaurant was traumatic for our foursome. It is disturbing to be an eyewitness to someone who is dying, but when that dying person unexpectedly returns to life without medical intervention, it is stunning. When Gloria and Bob drove away in the taxi, I could feel my level of adrenalin dropping as my breathing slowed down and my body stopped shaking. I knew something extraordinary had happened and that my life would never be quite the same.

I still do not completely understand why God put me and my son at the table with Gloria to experience one of the most supernatural moments of our lives. I do know that it was a unique privilege, and I'm thankful that God allowed my son to also be a witness to the miracle.

I have often wondered what became of Gloria and why God revived her. Perhaps He had a significant purpose for her life, so He placed me across the table from her as a channel through which He could deliver His healing power.

The miracle was one of those traumatic life events that probably cannot be fully comprehended this side of eternity.

I would not have volunteered for the job, but it was a great blessing to witness an example of God's amazing power and authority over life and death.

I would not have volunteered for the job, but it was a great blessing to witness an example of God's amazing power and authority over life and death.

Great Commission work is the perfect setting for clearly observing God work in miraculous ways that are undeniable. Missionaries have attested to this throughout the ages.

1. Why do God's power and presence feel more obvious in Great Commission settings?

2. How has God done something through you that you were entirely unqualified for and/or unprepared to do?

3. Describe a miracle that you have observed that can only be explained as a divine intervention.

SEVEN

The Stranger, the Sign, and the Sorrow

Rejoice with those who rejoice, and weep with those who weep.
(Romans 12:15 NKJV)

I didn't know that signs from God are sometimes written in all capital letters until I saw the vanity plate of the white Ford Expedition on the road ahead of me. The license plate caught my attention because it had been customized with the word "ROATAN." At the time, it was rare to find anyone in my world who knew about Roatán, Honduras, which is a small Caribbean island forty miles off the coast of Honduras. My son and I had just returned from the island.

On the last day of our vacation on Roatán, I woke up early for one last opportunity to snorkel in the world's second-largest barrier reef. My son had planned to snorkel with me, but he could not manage to drag his body out of bed. So, I tiptoed out of our beachfront cottage, hoping not to awaken him. Before I could step into the glistening turquoise water, a nondescript stranger on the beach asked me what I was doing on the island. I told him that I had just finished working at a large orphanage on the mainland and had come afterward to the island for rest and recuperation. The stranger, whom I had never seen before, told me I should come back to work at one of the orphanages on the island or teach English-language classes.

I was surprised to hear that the island paradise had orphanages. Later, I realized that his suggestion about teaching English-language classes was even more surprising. English-language development is my specialty, but the stranger could not have known that. It's not unusual to be stopped by people on the beach peddling goods or services, but the stranger was a giver, not a taker. The experience had a dreamlike quality that left me with a vivid memory of the spoken words, but only a vague recall about the man's physical appearance. I wish I had paid closer attention. At the time, I gave little value to the encounter, but in retrospect, I believe the stranger was a messenger, and I wonder if he was flesh and bones.

> *At the time, I gave little value to the encounter, but in retrospect, I believe the stranger was a messenger, and I wonder if he was flesh and bones.*

The scene of the stranger on the beach

Several hours later, my son and I were on our way to the airport with Omar, the taxi-cab driver. The radio in the taxi was a bit loud, with J. Vernon McGee preaching "Through the Bible" in his unmistakable Southern accent. Omar told us that the sermon was being broadcast from a radio station on the site of the Honduran-owned-and-operated orphanage in Gravel Bay. I asked Omar for more information about the island orphanages, and he told me there were two of them. He pointed out the American-owned-and-operated children's home as we drove through Sandy Bay.

It sounded appealing to come back and work at one of the orphanages on the island. I could avoid flying into the capital of Honduras, which is considered one of the most dangerous international airports in the world because of the surrounding mountainous terrain and the short runway. But I was certain that I could never justify Great Commission work on a beautiful cruise-ship destination like Roatán. Wouldn't that be wrong?

I had never done a mission trip to any place that was lovely like Roatán, so I dismissed the idea…until I returned home and saw the Roatán vanity plate in all capital letters directly in front of me! What a "coincidence" to see the license plate as I drove along the narrow street up a hill toward the small elementary school where I worked! It was my first day back at work to prepare for the new school year. I followed the white Expedition with the interesting license plate, which "just happened" to pull into my school parking lot. The driver parked in the nearly empty parking lot and was probably surprised by my avid interest in her license plate. She explained that she had met her husband on the island of Roatán while on a family vacation. They had married and lived on the island, but their plan had been to move to the United States when their little girl was old enough for school, because Honduran schools are mediocre. Their daughter was placed in my class.

Because of the stranger on the beach and the sign on the license plate, I had a shift in my thinking about Great Commission work on Roatán. I decided to research opportunities for ministry on the island and hoped to find work at one of the two orphanages. The children's home that was owned and operated by Hondurans did not have a website or any other way to contact the organization. I *was* able to connect with the director of the American-owned orphanage via the Internet. I received a phone call shortly thereafter from the man. He was enthusiastic about making plans for me to become involved at the children's home. I was thrilled about working at the orphanage and felt like God had come close to writing it in stone that I should do so.

At about the same time, I also made an online connection with an American who was the pastor of a Roatán church that was located near the American-owned orphanage. He exhorted me to stay away from the children's home because there was an ongoing power struggle between the director and the orphanage board. The pastor's warning brought me to a dead end. I was disappointed because I thought the sign on the license plate and the messenger on the beach were God's way of directing me to ministry on the island.

I began a dialogue with the American pastor about the possibility of teaching English-language classes at his church to attract people in the community for the purpose of evangelism. We came up with a plan that worked for both of us. I was excited about the assignment because there were indications that God was leading me to work on the island. I was certain that I had been set up for a special assignment.

The pastor of the church where I committed to teaching English-language classes was a multi-talented man. He owned and operated a church compound with hotel rooms, a café, a commercial-size kitchen, and a large meeting room where church services were held in both English and Spanish. The pastor had purchased an old hotel with the plan of converting it into a church compound with a hotel for visiting missionaries. He closed the real-estate deal on a trip to the island without his wife, but she didn't seem to mind. Afterward, they found out that there were major structural problems that were unknown to them at the time of sale. Church work teams came from the United States to help with the renovations.

The pastor and his family were all part of the ministry. Some of his married children and their spouses were also involved in the mission. After the remodeling was complete, missionaries started lodging in the inexpensive hotel rooms, and church services began. The pastor preached, and his sons led the worship songs. After services, a meal prepared by the pastor's wife and their adult children was offered to incentivize attendance at the church.

The pastor was more than just a preacher and innkeeper. He was also an expert in water purification, which was a very practical skill, considering the location. It was rare and wonderful to be able to drink the tap water at the church compound, especially since the hotel rooms would have been rated a two-star resort. The man also helped the nearby community by bringing them a safe source of drinking water.

Additionally, the pastor and his family became the temporary guardians of the orphans who lived at the American-operated children's home after the director was finally pressured into leaving and did so abruptly. For about two weeks, the pastor and his family lovingly sheltered the children at their church complex. They put them to bed in the hotel rooms and cared for them until the interim directors showed up.

The pastor and his big family were multi-talented and undaunted by their departure from the comforts of home. They had one daughter and five sons with names like Clayton and Carlton, plus other variations of boy names that sounded good with "ton" attached to the end. The youngest son was born in one of the small and rustic hotel rooms at the church complex.

The multi-talented Calvary Chapel pastor and his family, including their infant son, who was born at the church compound in Sandy Bay

The pastor and his family were also potters who created beautiful pottery to sell at the cafe. I suspect that when the man was young, he drove a van painted in psychedelic colors and his wife had long hair parted down the middle and adorned with flowers. Once you met the couple, you could guess they were probably from the wild and crazy state of California.

Whatever their past, they were born-again believers who had the obvious intention of sharing the Gospel with the islanders, regardless of the personal cost. I remember the pastor and his family explaining the way Murphy's Law prevailed on the island. They hired locals to help at the church compound, who stole from them. Their infant granddaughter ate rat poison and nearly died.

Because they were trying to manage so many different ministries, they informed all hotel guests upfront that they operated a yo-yo resort. That was an acronym for "you're on your own."

The pastor and his family were heavily invested in the church on Roatán. In addition to all the hard work in the hot, humid weather, they lived in an unsafe and poor community, drinking in the bitterness of the culture of poverty. They tried to help untangle a long list of serious problems among their church members, like unemployment, drug abuse, crime, prostitution, and incest. Suffering is universal to mankind, but it is more intense among the poor because of senseless problems like children who can't attend school for the lack of funds to purchase the required uniforms. The pastor and his family did not spend their entire career on the island,

Some friends joined me at the Calvary Chapel compound, and we met this little girl from the Sandy Bay Orphanage.

but during their substantial time of ministry, they enriched the lives of their little community in ways that will last for all eternity. The pastor and his family eventually returned to the United States, but they have remained involved with the church, mostly from afar. Few individuals would have lasted eight years laboring with such intensity. Their multi-faceted ministry must have worn them down and possibly shortened the duration of their mission work.

It was my privilege to teach English-language classes at Calvary Chapel Son Rise while the pastor and his family were still living at the church compound. However, it was a tough assignment. No one came to pick me up at the airport because of a misunderstanding. I was on my own to lug around heavy suitcases with all my classroom supplies and find a taxi from the airport to the church. I had not been accurate at estimating the weight of my check-in luggage prior to departure and, therefore, had to leave a big trash bag of supplies behind on the airport floor. Later, it worked to my advantage that I had been forced to lighten up my luggage.

Although it was not a great start, I was excited to set up my class-room and begin teaching. There was a strong interest in English-language classes. I had a caseload of sixty students throughout the day in a packed room where the air conditioning frequently failed. In addition to so many students, many small children came to class with their mothers. The sweet and humble students made me feel like all my efforts were appreciated and worthwhile.

Marie was my star student. She was the only student in my advanced class and also my favorite new friend. She was bright and sparkling with enthusiasm for life and for the precious life that she was carrying. Marie was very close to giving birth to her firstborn. She had a cheerful personality that made her a joy to everyone around her. She asked me to help her write a letter in English to her unborn child describing her deep love for the baby and her hopes and dreams for the child's future.

Shortly after we finished the sweet letter, Marie delivered her beloved firstborn. Tragically, the baby died. The memory still sparks deep emotion. The American pastor and his family com-passionately came alongside Marie, helping her with the burial arrangements. They provided a handcrafted wooden coffin for the baby. They showed me the first coffin lined with red satin, but it was too small. Marie gave birth to a large, fully developed baby boy. Sadly, the infant mortality rate in Honduras is three times higher than in the United States because women like Marie do not have access to adequate prenatal care.

The death of the baby and the grief that followed weighed heavily upon Marie and everyone who loved her. It was hard visiting her in the tiny, rustic dwelling where she and her artist husband lived. God did have plans for me on the island that year, but the plans were not what I had expected or wanted. I was not looking forward to seeing Marie, knowing that she would be consumed by her tragic circumstances. But I knew God wanted me to share in her mourning. His words in Romans 12:15 instruct us to share the sorrow and joy of others. Perhaps God wants us to grieve with others because when grief is shared, it helps the one experiencing unbearable loss to shed some of their sorrow because of the compassion of others who take away bits of the suffering.

I believe that God directed my path to Roatán that year because Marie would need one more person to share her massive pain. When I knocked on her door, I knew she would not be the same person I had grown to love, and that she would never be the same. She was alone and drowning in an ocean of sorrow. Perhaps I was sent there to be one more person to hold her head above the water.

> *Marie was loved by many, but it was a privilege to be among those who took away a shovelful of the mountain of grief that she could not carry alone.*

Marie had intense back pain from labor and childbirth, so I offered to give her a massage and also to pray for her. Human touch and prayer created a passageway through which God's love and healing could flow into the broken heart of a young woman who had come home from the maternity ward empty-handed. Marie was loved by many, but it was a privilege to be among those who took away a shovelful of the mountain of grief that she could not carry alone.

RUMINATIONS

When I saw "ROATAN" on the vanity license plate so soon after my encounter with the messenger on the beach, I took it as a sign. Some people believe in coincidences, but I'm more inclined to believe in divine appointments, signs, and wonders.

God used the American pastor on Roatán to guide me away from a bad situation at an orphanage and into a purposeful ministry at his church. The pastor and his family amazed me with their many skills and outreaches to the needy people in their community.

My favorite member of their community was Marie. Reaching out to her after her baby died was difficult because of the depth of her heartbreak and grief. Marie was undoubtedly the main reason God sent me to the island that year.

1. Describe a time in your life when God wanted you to do something full of purpose but also difficult or uncomfortable to accomplish.

2. What skills do you have that could be used for the Great Commission? Note: most people don't have multiple skills like the Roatán pastor in this chapter.

3. Describe how *you* become burned out. How can burnout be avoided?

Calvary Chapel Son Rise

EIGHT

Mutiny and the Underage Insurgents

You are my hiding place; You, LORD, protect me from trouble; You
surround me with songs and shouts of deliverance. Selah.
(Psalm 32:7)

Teaching English-language classes on the island felt purposeful,
but I didn't really want to teach English-language classes. I
wanted to work at one of the orphanages. When the problems at the
American-owned children's home were resolved, the pastor at the
Roatán church informed me that it would be acceptable to contact
the new directors. When I connected with them, they welcomed
my offer of help at the orphanage.

When I returned to Roatán, I felt like I was supposed to be back
on the island, doing the thing that the messenger on the beach had
encouraged me to do. The new interim directors asked me to bring
rat traps and prenatal pills, which led me to believe it was going
to be an interesting adventure. I fell in love with the children, even
though they were the wildest bunch of kids I had ever met. To this
day, I am Facebook friends with several of the grown-up children.

Britt and Tammy were the new directors. They were kind and
loving to the children, but they readily admitted that they did not
know how to control the fourteen kids they were desperately trying
to parent. Neither of them had ever had children of their own.

Tammy was a marriage and family therapist, but her credentials did nothing to rein in the unruly little monsters.

The wild things at the playground

The directors couldn't even convince the children to sit quietly at the table for meals. It was ridiculous but entertaining. The boys and girls would jump from table to table, ignoring the adults who wanted to ensure the children could eat their meals without choking on their food.

The children were less difficult to manage outdoors. The daily routine at the orphanage was to walk across the street and play on the beach, as we were eaten alive by sand fleas, otherwise known as *no-see-ums*. There were so many of the pesky biting insects that sometimes you *could* see them in what looked like a swirling cloud of fog. Sometimes when we were at the beach, we would collect buckets full of *craboo*, mangoes, and sea grapes. Geraldo would amaze us by fearlessly climbing up the tall palm trees to fetch coconuts.

At the time, the orphanage was not well established, and they needed help because of the tumultuous upheaval at the home the previous year. The founding directors, who were the only houseparents that the children had ever known, had left abruptly after seven years. The young and inexperienced interim houseparents who replaced them had to deal with twice-orphaned children. The directors were exhausted and needed a serious chunk of rest and recuperation. The wife was having a difficult first trimester of pregnancy, so her husband was carrying the majority of the responsibilities at the children's home.

Our team of three kept the children occupied so the houseparents could have some time to breathe. We filled up time before and after school with walks to the beach, Bible stories, singing,

and crafts, and we also helped with homework. The cook had Sunday mornings off, so we had fun in the kitchen making Mickey Mouse pancakes and other fun breakfast meals for the boys and girls. We completed a post-construction cleanup project in one of the

We taught the children about the plagues of Egypt

volunteer apartments, which had the remains of a rat infestation. Afterward, we set the rat traps that we had brought from home.

The interim houseparents asked me to do one thing that I was uncomfortable with, but I am terrible at saying no. Plus, I had been trained as a short-term missionary to step out of my comfort zone, be flexible, and do whatever was needed to the best of my ability. I don't think the directors realized what they were asking someone with my driving skills to do. Britt asked me to drive the students back and forth to school in an extra-long van. I wanted to tell him that I couldn't parallel park my mid-size sedan to save my soul. But I accepted the job. There were morning and

Jumping off the dock across the street from the orphanage

afternoon sessions in order to double the use of the school sites. The day began at 5:30 AM with a lot of driving into the congested town of Coxen Hole. I also drove a rambunctious three-year-old to a nearby preschool.

> *If you didn't disconnect the battery at night, the orphanage van wouldn't start the next morning. Guess who forgot to disconnect the battery one night.*

The van was a hunk of junk. The windshield wipers didn't work, which made driving in the tropical climate a challenge. The island roads were poorly maintained and dangerous when the streets were wet. No one bothered rolling up the van windows when it rained, because the van leaked water from the roof whether the windows were up or down. You couldn't keep your foot on the accelerator for very long because whatever was supposed to shield the engine heat from the driver's foot was missing. If you didn't disconnect the battery at night, the orphanage van wouldn't start the next morning. Guess who forgot to disconnect the battery one night. The kids were thrilled at the thought of not going to school, but my kind pastor friend from Calvary Chapel Son Rise came to give us a jumpstart.

I quickly realized that driving on the island was a blood sport. I later found out that if you spend enough time driving there, you are either going to be run off the road or be involved in an accident. In the event of an accident, the person with the highest net worth is probably going to be blamed and also extorted for repairs and medical costs, especially if that driver is a gringo.

Most residents on the island are too poor to own a car, but for those who do, vehicles are mostly uninsured. This is problematic because of the dangers of navigating the narrow, winding roads with no shoulders and occasional drop-offs without safety barriers. I drove about in the extra-long van with fear and trembling.

The horrible condition of the van and the roads were not the worst part of my driving responsibility. My instructions were to pick up students from a morning session of school in Coxen Hole and then drive them back in the opposite direction without stopping as

Samara the schoolgirl, and behind her, the bad excuse for a van

we drove past the orphanage. These no-stop driving instructions were necessary to deliver a girl on time to an afternoon session at a different school beyond the orphanage. This created a huge problem with several of the older boys, who strongly preferred to be dropped off at the orphanage when I drove by.

One day, as we were approaching the children's home without plans to stop, the intimidating gang threatened to jump out of the moving vehicle if I didn't stop to drop them off at the orphanage. I told them Britt had instructed me

not to stop or Samara would be late for her afternoon class. They didn't like Britt's instructions. As we were approaching the orphanage, Raffi slid open the van door and threatened to jump if I didn't stop. Then he proceeded to tell the other boys to toss their backpacks out of the open door before they jumped from the van. No one was wearing seatbelts because, of course, there were no seatbelts in the dilapidated van.

I was stressed and conflicted and indecisive. Should I follow orders from the director or play it safe and acquiesce to the demand of the older boys? In retrospect, I should have dropped off the boys, but I kept driving and praying and watching for flying backpacks, while simultaneously driving a van full of children wearing no seatbelts with the sliding door wide open.

Providentially, no backpacks flew out the open door, and some sort of supernatural superglue kept everyone's backsides on the seats of our bad excuse for a van. I pulled off the main road to deliver Samara to her afternoon session of school, so relieved that everyone was safe and sound that it didn't even matter to me that the older boys finally did jump out of the van, walking off with parting words that were not in the textbooks of my college Spanish classes. I must say I was glad the monstrous teenagers were no longer my passengers. I knew they would be late for lunch and would have to walk quite a distance back to the orphanage in the hot and humid weather with their heavy backpacks. These boys later apologized to me and never again threatened to jump out of the van.

RUMINATIONS

I did not know in advance that my first assignment at the American-owned orphanage was going to be a battle. There was a vacuum of power at the children's home, with numerous individuals vying for the vacant position of authority.

The board of directors had just wrested control of the orphanage back from a man who then suddenly departed after seven years as CEO and father to the children.

Unlike Orphanage Emmanuel, where we lived in separate quarters from the hundreds of children, we were living among fourteen young insurgents who took no prisoners.

Our mission team of three needed reinforcements. We were outnumbered by an army of underage renegades who refused to bow to the leadership of adults. Unlike our assignment at Orphanage Emmanuel, where we lived in separate quarters from the hundreds of children, here we were living among fourteen young insurgents who took no prisoners. We were in the trenches. Our only relief came when night fell and the children slept.

We were initiated into the children's world of brokenness caused by abandonment—first by their biological parents and then by their dearly departed houseparents, who had been the center of their universe for the previous seven years.

The rogue orphans decided we needed to be drafted into their army and put through boot camp to bring us into submission to their authority. The children were formidable soldiers who were not going to be easily reined in during our short three-week stay.

However, we decided to take back some enemy territory. War is hellish, and we died on several hills. We decided to choose our battles. We needed to demonstrate both love and strength. We barely survived.

The interim houseparents were thoroughly spent and planned to jump ship the moment replacements arrived. Our team negotiated a fragile truce in the guerrilla warfare in order to give the exhausted interim houseparents a well-deserved break until replacements arrived. We even pulled off a foot washing event for the children to demonstrate their appreciation to the houseparents for all their tender loving care.

The truce was weak when the children were shuttled back and forth to school. I had reluctantly agreed to be the driver of the extra-long van. My rebellious passengers pushed the limits of my patience and driving skills. It was especially hard to stand my ground with the teen boys, who functioned as generals in the kiddie army (not to mention the fact that they were bigger than me). I was weak, but God was strong.

When one of the older boys slid open the van door and it looked like some of his followers were going to jump out of our moving vehicle, my decision to keep driving could have ended very badly. I was weak, but God was strong.

Our team was clearly in over our heads. It was a good thing that the battle did not belong to us. We were naturally good at nurturing but not so good at fighting. We came to the orphanage to love the children, not to subdue the little rebels. We walked into a virtual power struggle with children who were good at waging war against the adult world that had gravely disappointed them. It was a battle that we didn't want to fight, but the alternative was anarchy.

Thankfully, the outcome of the battle did not depend on *our* ability to wage war. God saved us all from what could have been some serious collateral damage. We were weak, but He was strong.

1. Describe a frightening trial in your life when you made it through the storm because although you were weak, God was strong.

2. Why is it important to be vigilant and well prepared for spiritual battle at all times, but especially on the mission field?

3. What is the meaning of Ephesians 6:11 regarding the armor of God?

Gathering *craboo*, a sweet yellow fruit

NINE

THE COUP AND THE PRESIDENT'S PAJAMAS

He makes nations great, and He destroys them; He enlarges nations, and leads them away. (Job 12:23)

On June 28, 2009, the world was looking at the country of Honduras with great interest. President Manuel Zelaya had attempted to trifle with his country's constitution. The Supreme Court consequently issued a secret warrant for his arrest, authorizing members of the army to storm his residence in the middle of the night. Masked soldiers pulled the president from his bed, took his cell phone, forced him into a van, and then flew him on a military transport to Costa Rica, where they left him standing on the runway in his pajamas.

Tanks patrolled the streets, military planes flew overhead, soldiers armed with large rifles were visible on the streets in large numbers, and there was a blackout of news on television and radio stations. Electricity, phone, and cable TV were cut or blocked nationwide. Public transportation was suspended.

No one could have predicted with certainty what the future held for the country. I had planned my annual mission trip to Honduras several months in advance of these events. My bags were packed. But I did not know what to do when friends and family called to tell me about the coup. With only a few days remaining prior to my departure, I was under time pressure to figure out what the Lord wanted me to do. I checked with the Honduran orphanage director, and he did not think I should cancel my trip.

The State Department was warning Americans to defer all non-essential travel to Honduras. I considered my assignment to be essential. It would be my first time as the temporary managing director of a children's home in Honduras. The new orphanage director and his family hadn't had a break in ten months. I had committed to filling in for them to enable the family to rest and recuperate from their difficult job. I had never before registered my Central American trips with the State Department—however, this year was an exception.

My assignment was on Roatán, which is an island about forty miles off the coast of Honduras. Without a doubt, there is a vast difference between the island and the mainland. The Honduran government has a vested interest in keeping the island as safe as possible for visitors because of the significant amount of taxes generated by tourism. The tourist areas on Roatán are a much different and safer place than the mainland.

Four days after the president of Honduras was flown out of the country against his will, I arrived for a short-term-mission assignment. As I descended the mobile airplane staircase onto the tarmac, I saw a woman who had stopped to take a photo of the soldiers who were on the roof of the airport building with big automatic rifles hanging over their shoulders. I thought about snapping a photo too, but I wanted to avoid drawing attention to myself. My plan was to keep a low profile and avoid all things political. I didn't talk in public unless it was necessary because my English identified me as an American, and the U.S. Secretary of State had spoken out against the coup. I obeyed the national curfew that restricted activity after dark, and I cringed when other Americans told me they were ignoring the government mandate.

Shortly after my arrival, someone told me that all Americans had been ordered to return home by the State Department. I was relieved to hear that the news was false. But people were edgy because no one knew for sure if the present situation would deteriorate into a textbook example from Central American history of bloody coups. During my assignment at the orphanage, the airlines were offering one-way exit flights for expats and early return flights for tourists, without a financial penalty for itinerary changes.

I knew this was going to be a year to remember. I arrived in advance of the other two team members to rest from the red-eye flight and prepare for my work at the orphanage. Before moving in at the children's home, I stayed at the nearby Calvary Chapel Son Rise Mission Inn with my friends and their five sons. I was thrilled when they told me that a large mission team needed all available hotel rooms on the main road, so I would have to be relocated to their waterfront condo.

> *It had an ugly pagan appearance with a dark aura that was palpable. It immediately made me feel uncomfortable and I knew I could not sleep in the condo if the monstrosity remained inside.*

The first thing I noticed in the condo was a copy of *yaba ding ding*, which is local slang for pre-Columbian artifacts that are sold in Honduras as souvenirs. The phony artifact in my condo was being used as a decorative interior doorstop. It had an ugly pagan appearance with a dark aura that was palpable. It immediately made me feel uncomfortable, and I knew I could not sleep in the condo if the monstrosity remained inside. I put it outdoors as far away as possible on the small front porch, facing away from the condo. Oddly enough, the next morning it was close to the front door and facing the condo as if it wanted back inside. I took the hideous thing to the pastor at the inn and explained my concerns. He informed me that the condo had previously been occupied by a young missionary couple who had purchased the artifact and left it behind. The couple had been plagued by various problems, including some serious medical issues, which forced them to abandon their assignment and return home.

Peggy Stranges was my next-door neighbor at the condo. She is the unofficial matron saint of the island because of the medical clinic that she founded. The facility in Sandy Bay provides free or affordable access to medical care for the poor islanders who live behind the scenes of the tourist attractions. The islanders call her medical center "Peggy's Clinic," but the sign in front says Clinica Esperanza. The clinic offers many opportunities for ministry, from counting pills to serving as a medical doctor. Some tourists who come on the cruise ships check the Internet for the clinic's list of needs and bring the items to donate during their visits to the island.

After a few days, my team members arrived, and I said farewell to Peggy and the people at the Mission Inn. We traveled a short distance to the orphanage to begin our assignment. It was good that my friend with nursing skills came along for the adventure. Shortly after our assignment began, my friend was able to assess the injury of one of the staff members. There was a sudden scream, so I ran to see if I could help. This young staff member was on the ground after falling down an outdoor staircase. It turned out to be only a sprain, and I was glad that I had seen

Injured staff member

crutches during my tour with the director prior to his departure. The staff member was treated with pain relievers and an ice pack. As a result of the accident, one of four on-site employees was partly disabled, and she was the primary caregiver for the baby at the orphanage.

The event made me realize that I needed to make it a priority to find the key to the vehicle that was available for emergencies. I was left with no medical-emergency instructions and no working cell phone, and the landline at the orphanage was unreliable.

The day before the director left with his family, two brothers were brought to the orphanage. The director was busy preparing for the family trip to the mainland, so we helped the boys settle in to their new home. The brothers were less needy than most new arrivals, but new residents need a lot of tender loving care and guidance. They usually come with only the clothes on their backs, so they need a new wardrobe, toiletries, and fresh linens on their beds.

I was faced with several administrative challenges. I handed out paychecks (all of which bounced), locked up the facility at night, documented family visitations, and fixed problems that made their way to me because nobody else was able to solve them.

The on-site groundskeeper came to me with a request for an unplanned and sudden leave of absence because his brother had been killed on the mainland. When I approved his request to leave and support his family, it meant we were down one more full-time staff member.

One night, a police car showed up with flashing lights, and I was so mentally exhausted that my first thought was that the police were going to arrest me because I had no credentials for my job and I wasn't a Honduran citizen. They had no intention of arresting me. Instead, they brought us an underage teenager that they had found in a bar. Fortunately, the injured staff member still had a few minutes of prepaid service left on her cell phone. I called the orphanage director, and he talked me through the admission procedure. The teenage girl was from the mainland and had nowhere to shelter on the island. The police wanted the orphanage to care for her until her eighteenth birthday, which was later in the year. The director asked me to look at the teenager and make an assessment of her character—more specifically, if she looked like a prostitute and if she might be a threat to the safety of the other children. He told me he would stay on the line while I took a look at the girl. I've never been a great judge of character, but I took a long, hard look. Being ignorant about the unique appearance of prostitutes, I felt unqualified to answer the director's questions. The police helped me out and told me that they did not think she was a prostitute, nor did they consider her to be a physical threat to the other children.

Still, the orphanage director was uncomfortable with the teenager staying under the same roof as the rest of us and advised me to place her in a small apartment that was separate from the main house. The apartment was locked, and the key was not on the huge keyring that I had been given. By this time, it was dark, and someone needed to climb in through the unlocked front window of the apartment. I asked the police officers for a flashlight, but they didn't have one, so I had to run upstairs to grab one of my own. I climbed through the window while the police watched me land ungracefully inside the unfurnished apartment, even though I was old enough to be their mother.

We set up our newest resident in the apartment and brought her a mattress, linens, toiletries, water, and snacks. I wanted her to feel welcome, so we chatted for a while. Then I prayed with the girl and gave her a good-night hug. She seemed harmless enough to me. Afterward, I hurried back to the main house, trying to avoid the mosquitoes that came out in greater numbers after dusk.

The next day, I was told that we were out of powdered baby formula. Someone had to go to the store to fetch some. I was the only able-bodied adult available who knew where the store was located. Unfortunately, I was unable to find the key to the van, so I started walking toward the store. The first vehicle that passed me stopped and gave me a lift. The driver was an American building contractor who filled my ear with his opinion about the coup. He told me that foreigners who owned real estate on the island were glad about the coup because they thought that President Zelaya was on a pathway to socialism, influenced by his friend Hugo Chavez, the president of Venezuela. My driver/contractor friend believed that real estate would have been nationalized if the exiled president had achieved his goals. This nice man drove me to the store and told me how to find a ride back to the orphanage with the baby formula.

I made it back to the orphanage before the baby cried for her next bottle of formula. However, it felt like we were putting out one fire after another. Our days began early in the morning and ended late at night. Only three of the children spoke English fluently, and I had limited Spanish skills. Before I left for Honduras, my mother had told me that she thought I was becoming too old for mission work. Her words kept ricocheting around inside my head.

When the director and his family returned from their vacation, I knew I was physically exhausted, but I didn't realize that my emotional tank was on zero. My two cautious team members had decided to fly home after our assignment was finished instead of staying for our planned vacation. When the cab driver picked me up from the orphanage to take me to the resort, I got into the car and started crying as soon as we drove off. I cried for a long time. My old friend Omar was the cab driver. He worked for the resort where I usually stayed and was the same cab driver that had originally pointed out the orphanage to my son and me on our ride to the airport. He must have been uncomfortable when he saw how I was processing my assignment only minutes after I walked away from my responsibilities. "Oh, the orphanage must be a hard place to work," he said in a compassionate voice. His kind words were comforting, but they felt like an understatement of my first attempt as a substitute director of a children's home in Central America during a military coup.

The staff, the team, and most of the children
during the summer of the coup

RUMINATIONS

Mission work is never going to be without risk. I probably would not have committed to substituting for the orphanage directors had I known that the dates of my mission were going to coincide with a military coup. I reasoned that there would be little fallout from the coup out on the island.

The soldiers with big rifles hanging over their shoulders on the airport roof upon my arrival were disconcerting. The new coup government was responding harshly toward protestors in the streets on the mainland, arresting thousands, beating others, and killing at least twenty people. This immediately decimated the tourist industry on the island, causing widespread unemployment. A crime spree came on the heels of the unemployment, including violent robberies and killings, some against tourists and American expats. I planned to stay on the orphanage grounds and leave only in an emergency.

My concern about an emergency at the orphanage under my watch was closer to home and distracted me from the overshadowing insecurity of the coup. We were left without any sort of medical-emergency plans. Additionally, we were without transportation because we were not given a key to the van. When the young woman who fed the baby informed me that there was no more baby formula, somebody had to go shopping.

It was annoying to have to go out shopping because someone had not left us well stocked with essential supplies. I especially did not want to be out walking along the main road in the hot, humid weather during a military coup.

Fortunately, I had good training for missions under Andrae's leadership. He had encouraged us to be flexible and do what needed to be done, even if we didn't want to do it or thought we didn't have the skills for the task. So, when the baby needed formula and there was no key to be found, I needed to be flexible and do something a bit risky and out of my comfort zone. I started walking down the long driveway to the main road and then headed toward the store, hoping to catch a ride with a passing cab. The taxi drivers on Roatán are not always safe, so I readily accepted a ride with a stranger who happened to be an American. I believe God sent him to me. At first, I thought he was an angel, but an angel probably would have waited around for me to shop and then taken me back to the children's home. I was extremely grateful that he pulled over and gave me a safe ride before I had walked very far.

> *At first, I thought he was an angel, but an angel probably would have waited around for me to shop and then taken me back to the children's home.*

The orphanage was unfenced at that time and felt like an unsafe place to be, especially under the circumstances and after dark. The directors had discontinued the armed guard that used to patrol the grounds at night. The only man who was expected to be on location during our assignment had left to support his family on the mainland.

Both of my team members decided to leave as soon as our mission was complete due to pressure from a fiancé and husband at home who were following the news about the political turmoil in Honduras.

It was a joy and a relief when the director and his family finally returned to the orphanage. I am not gifted administratively, so my first attempt as the substitute director during a military coup was draining. I was thankful for God's protection and His provision of all our needs.

1. Why is flexibility an important component of the Great Commission?
2. Why is mission work a place where we need to lean heavily upon the Lord?
3. Why does God sometimes ask missionaries to go to unsafe places in the world?

TEN

BROTHERS, BAND-AIDS, AND BROKEN HEARTS

I had fainted, unless I had believed to see the goodness of the LORD in the land of the living. (Psalm 27:13 KJV)

The year of the coup in Honduras was a tough assignment. The ousting of the sitting president complicated life in the nation and increased the level of poverty, but the fallout from the coup was minimal by the standards of Central American history. I'm glad I did not cancel my ministry plans that year because, as difficult as it was, it turned out to be a great blessing and privilege to work at the orphanage in 2009.

Great Commission work is always going to be full of challenges. The work is usually not easy or convenient, but it is an open invitation to divine appointments, privileges, and blessings. We live in an upside-down world where it can be difficult to discern the pathway to blessings, and too often, we look for them in the wrong places. We all want blessings. They are readily found in Great Commission work.

When God directed me to accept an offer to be the substitute director for the first time at the Roatán orphanage, I knew my lack of executive skills meant I would be skating on thin ice unless I leaned heavily upon God. He enabled me to function beyond my capabilities and complete the job.

An orphanage board member had contacted me asking if I would fill in for the houseparents because they had been at their post for ten months and needed some rest and recuperation. I did not have confidence in myself to complete the assignment, and I knew that it would be an enormous undertaking for someone with my lack of administrative skills. Being uninformed about the amount of physical labor the job would demand, I went with too few team members. When the coup and other factors were thrown into the mix, my only hope was in God's power to make up for my weakness. When two of the resident staff members were taken out of commission by odd circumstances, I knew my assignment would be impossible without God's help. I would have surely failed and fainted from exhaustion had it not been for "the goodness of the LORD in the land of the living" (Psalm 27:13 KJV).

The difficulty of the job did not eclipse the beauty and blessing that accompanied the hard work. Two of the dearest little boys were brought to the orphanage when I "just happened" to be on-site for eighteen days of the 365-day calendar year. The brothers were six and eight years old. Like most of the children who arrive at the children's home for the first time, the boys came with nothing but the clothes on their backs. It was my privilege to gather clothing and personal items for them, set them up in their new bedroom, and tuck them into bed that first night. Surely, their own mother wanted to be present to hold the little boys and kiss them good night, but in her absence, God had arranged for me to be in that place at that time to stand in for their mother. An affectionate grandma type was a good fit in that unique situation, and I was that made-for-the-occasion substitute mommy. It was such a tender time, and

> *Like most of the children who arrive at the children's home for the first time, the boys came with nothing but the clothes on their backs.*

the opportunity was pure sweetness to my soul. I'm sure it was the primary reason that I was sent to Roatán during the dreaded year of the coup.

Yadir was the elder brother and the earthly anchor of his little brother's soul. He was one of those self-governing children with a natural bent toward the straight-and-narrow path. He had natural leadership skills and a servant's heart.

His little brother had a different temperament. Alejandro was as cute and lovable as his big brother, but he had a propensity to push the limits of acceptable behavior while remaining in everyone's good graces. He was a profession-al-soccer-player wannabe, and if speed is the essential ingredient for that, he will someday outper-form Carlos Pavón. On his first day at the orphanage, Alejandro performed a disappearing act with such precision that he seemed to vanish into thin air.

The brothers were unusual in that they did not appear to be in distress like many new arrivals at the children's home. There was a notably strong brotherly bond

Young Yadir deep in thought

between the two boys, which probably buffered the trauma. From the beginning, the boys appeared to be unbroken. They probably had a loving mother, possibly a woman stuck in a trap that she thought she couldn't escape before the authorities removed her children from her arms. The boys had older sisters who came to visit them when they first arrived, but then rarely if ever visited them thereafter. In the culture of the Honduran Bay Islands, big sisters often function like second mothers. These brothers may have been pleasant and somewhat well-balanced children because of the additional love and nurturing of their older sisters.

The brothers' second day at the children's home was full of new types of activities for the boys. The changing of the guard was in process, as the houseparents were finishing up my orientation and preparing to leave. It was a busy time, and no one was paying much attention to the well-behaved new arrivals. Before the houseparents left, the younger brother somersaulted down a full flight of tall stairs. I "just happened" to be near the bottom of the stairs when he tumbled from the top all the way to the bottom of the wooden staircase. I watched with horror, expecting Alejandro to be seriously injured. It was astounding to see him quickly stand, smile, and say, "I'm okay!" as if nothing had happened. He had only a few scratches. I had been planted there at that time to tenderly clean his wounds and put Band-Aids on his minor injuries.

The brothers with their assembled LEGO spacecraft

It was odd that a boy with obvious athletic skills and agility had tumbled down the stairs. Perhaps tall staircases were unfamiliar to him. He and his brother were from a smaller nearby island where Christopher Columbus had once landed. Most of the buildings and homes on the island had been destroyed by Hurricane Mitch two years before Yadir was born. The island infrastructure was unsophisticated, and rebuilding after the disaster was slow because natural resources for reconstruction were scarce. At the time of this writing, there was still only a single two-mile-long road and about 5,500 inhabitants on the island. When Yadir was five years old, there were only three cars on the entire island. Most transportation is still by boat, using the canals on the island, giving the place the nickname of "the Venice of Honduras." There is a channel on the island called the Canal, which gives access from the north all the way to the south of the island. The primary source of income for the islanders is fishing, and I can imagine the boys in their tropical setting, paddling their own homemade vessel and catching the evening meal for the family.

The boys grew up on white-sand streets and waterways that meandered through mangrove forests. The brothers undoubtedly had many adventures interacting with the island wildlife in their tropical childhood playground. Once, there was a boa constrictor on the orphanage premises that needed to be eliminated because it was potentially dangerous to the smaller children. Yadir took care of the monstrous serpent, while the other children and adults watched in fear. Most people I know run in the opposite direction of boa constrictors; Yadir knew how to handle the beast with confidence.

The extensive pavement at the orphanage was unlike the native stomping grounds where the boys had lived. Transportation with wheels was rare in their hometown, so they were inexperienced with skateboards. The older brother saw the other children at the orphanage riding skateboards on their bellies down a gentle cement incline. He joined the fun but soon lost some skin when he fell off the skateboard onto his face. A small part of his eyebrow was missing. He didn't lose a lot of skin, but the eyebrow area is not designed to take blunt force. Once again, I "just happened" to be close enough to witness the injury of one of the brothers. When I disinfected what was similar to a small burn, Yadir was unflinching. It was good that God put me close by when Yadir was injured. Without my presence, he probably would have carried

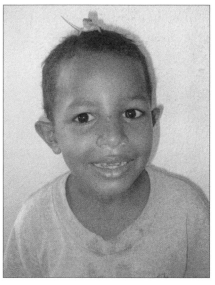

Alejandro with a gecko on his head

on without any first-aid treatment, thus risking infection. I think I was supposed to be there at that moment in time to administer the necessary first aid. I could tell he had not previously been coddled and fussed over when injured. Yadir had experienced life in a way that had developed remarkable bravery and courage for a boy his age.

When I left my home in 2009 to work at the orphanage, I did not know that God was sending me to put Band-Aids on brothers because their own mother was no longer available to do so. It was a divine appointment and a blessing to be a part of God's provision of tender loving care for the boys. Ten years later, I asked Yadir what it had felt like when he first arrived at the orphanage. He said, "It felt like home." I was surprised by his quick response because of the circumstances that preceded his admission to the children's home and the injuries that occurred shortly after the arrival of the brothers. Miraculously, God's goodness broke through the lament of losing his home and family of origin.

I didn't know the brothers would show up at the orphanage with a hole in their hearts because they had abruptly lost their mother. But when they arrived, I clearly understood my purpose and God's will for my life. When I tucked the boys into bed at night, I knew that I was exactly where God wanted me to be, doing precisely the thing He wanted me to do. Someday, heaven will clearly reveal the perfect will of God for us. Until then, front-line mission work is a thrilling preview of that glorious revelation.

> *Someday, heaven will clearly reveal the perfect will of God for us. Until then, front-line mission work is a thrilling preview of that glorious revelation.*

RUMINATIONS

God's timing can feel frustrating because it tends to be out of synchronization with the timing we desire. However, in Great Commission work, the perfection of His timing is more clearly understood and embraced.

The brothers have a special place in my heart, probably because God's timing allowed me to be the first person at the orphanage to help them through the nightmare of transitioning from their home of origin to their new group home. God's timing and purpose for my life seemed crystal clear as I welcomed the boys to their new home. More than a decade later, the boys are young men, and we still have a connection that I hope will last my lifetime.

Great Commission work is full of purpose, but it is also full of many unknowns. Circumstances arise that are impossible to anticipate. In my experience, there are always detours from my original plans and the detours tend to be closer to God's plans. Often what we think will be the main thing ends up being a minor thing or vice versa. The unknowns are not fully appreciated until after the unknowns become known.

Expectations for Great Commission work are often unfulfilled, possibly because we do not have God's perspective. Or possibly because if we knew what was awaiting us on the mission field, we would remain at home, safe and sound. Sometimes ignorance *is* bliss.

1. Why is the will of God more obvious to us during Great Commission work than when we are living our routine lives at home?

2. Why is God's timing easier to appreciate while on the mission field?

3. Why is Great Commission work an open invitation to divine appointments, privileges, and blessings?

4. What is your purpose in life?

ELEVEN

TÍA THE GREAT

Well done, good and faithful servant. (Matthew 25:23)

One of the many enjoyable benefits of Great Commission work is connecting with extraordinary people. It has been a privilege to befriend and labor alongside a woman who is affectionately called "Tía" by the children who love her. *Tía* means "aunt" in Spanish, but in the culture of Roatán, it has a richer meaning than the English equivalent. For the children at the orphanage, it would be better translated as "Mommy." Tía was the heart of the children's home, where she served the Lord and the children at the orphanage starting June 29, 2009. She has a heart like Jesus's. There is no one like her, and to the children at the home, there will never, ever be anyone like her, because she was the closest thing to a real mother they had ever known. Kind and compassionate, she held together the broken hearts of her beloved children. When children would first arrive at the orphanage, they would sometimes shadow Tía until they felt safe enough to venture beyond her warmth and security. When babies arrived, she would feed them, change them, bathe them, and hold them close.

Tía functioned as the unofficial and underpaid CEO at the orphanage, with the heart of a servant. She is the devoted mother of four adult children, all capable and lovable individuals. Along with her husband and children, she is an example of the Biblical model of a family unit in a culture where this is uncommon. Tía and her family have been a valuable source of blessing to the children and staff at the home. Her husband was a taxi driver, so she arranged safe transportation for the children and staff. When the boys needed their hair trimmed, she had one of her sons stop by to give haircuts.

Tía's executive skills brought a sense of order and stability to the children's home. I met Tía the second time I was the substitute director at the orphanage. What a difference one person

> *What a difference one person with administrative skills and a heart for the children can make!*

with administrative skills and a heart for the children can make! It made my job more doable. No more hitching a ride to the store for baby formula or other essentials, because Tía kept the place well stocked and organized. When we *were* low on supplies, Tía shopped for us. During my assignment, Tía had everything under control while she was on-site six days a week, and she was on call during her day off. She was willing to spend the night or work longer hours if necessary. Tía's presence was comforting, and having her available 24/7 took away the stress of managing the orphanage while the director was on leave. Tía minimized the side effects of being a substitute director and kept everything running well, regardless of who was at the helm.

Tía was the one devoted constant in the life of the children who lived at the children's home. She was heaven sent to the boys and girls, and she filled them up with faith and love. Throughout the years, she was a dependable channel through which the love of Jesus flowed into the lives of so many abandoned children. She treated the kids like they were her own and bragged about them on social media.

Tía is a saint. She is not like other women—she is a real-life, modern-day wonder woman. Some women make it to hero status for daily plodding along and doing the same-old hard work day after day, setting aside their own personal desires and pouring themselves into the lives of others. Some make singular acts of great sacrifice. She qualifies as a hero on both accounts, and she did it for the "least of these," who had nothing to give in return. I have a crazy hope that one of the kids will someday grow up and achieve millionaire or celebrity status and then come back to honor and reward her for her goodness!

Someone once told me that Tía was the glue that held the orphanage together. I immediately understood. Tía was originally hired to be the cook. That would be a full-time job for most of us. Not for Tía. At barely over five feet tall and probably a hundred pounds, she was a dynamo but completely under control! Once, I walked into the kitchen, and she was wielding a huge meat cleaver above her head. It came down in one fell swoop, splitting a partially frozen chicken in half. The woman would be dangerous if she were the enemy!

There was something about Tía's demeanor that commanded more respect than a woman of her stature and gender would normally receive in her culture. I have a feeling she may have had wilder

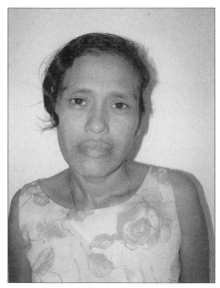

Tía the Great

days—who knows? I will always wonder about the gold star on her right front tooth. She looks like a Hispanic version of Angelina Jolie, and she dressed impeccably in a dress or skirt for work. She made me wish I could speak Spanish fluently so I could hear her life story straight from her own lips.

When I substituted for the director, I let everyone know that if Tía was around, she was the real boss. Everyone knew that, even if I didn't defer to her. The boys and girls naturally looked to her for guidance because she was the de facto caregiver and guardian of the children. I dreaded her one day a week off.

Tía was not only productive; she was intuitive about the needs of the children. She seemed to know what was in the heart of every child. She was wise about who had been wronged and who was in the wrong, who needed to apologize and who needed to forgive, and who needed a tear wiped away. The orphanage shelters twenty-plus boys and girls, which requires someone who is brilliant at the fine art of refereeing. She was skilled at stopping altercations before they happened but also good at untangling disagreements after they erupted. Tía had the discernment, decisiveness, and authoritative presence to skillfully execute her judgments in a way that was both merciful and just.

Tía making delicious pupusas

Tía's life revolved around the needs of the children at the orphanage. When they needed to be fed, she fixed them tasty meals on time and on a shoestring budget. She excelled at baking and grilling. She also made the best homemade tamales, pastelitos, baleadas, pupusas, and tortillas. Sometimes she went crab hunting on her days off to provide crab soup for the boys and girls. Feeding large groups was her forte. Her signature chicken and rice dish was a crowd pleaser on beach days.

Tía had a remarkable work ethic, and she was a golden example of this to the children. She was energetic and carried the workload of several people. It was obvious that her work was more of a ministry than a job. During her work schedule of six days a week, she accomplished the majority of the total workload at the orphanage while she was on-site. She somehow managed to bring children into the kitchen and train them to be productive instead of underfoot. Most of the children enjoyed being in the kitchen with Tía and knew how to pull their weight as kitchen helpers. I donated numerous potato peelers because there never seemed to be enough of them for all of her willing and capable helpers at large feedings, like quinceañeras, graduations, and when large teams showed up. She never complained about the heat in the kitchen, the rats, the ever-present cockroaches in the drawers and cupboards, and the massive effort it took to feed and clean up after so many people!

Tía was passionate about loving and nurturing all of the children that God brought under her authority. First, she won their love and respect, and then she had them eating out of her hand of mercy.

Her exemplary style of nurturing was noticeable in the way she treated the children like image-bearers of God. She used her rank at the top of the chain of command to set an example of kind and courteous social interaction and insisted that the children do the same. She knew how to turn rough-and-tumble teenage boys into gentle playmates for toddlers. From the top down, she set the tone of humble other-centeredness and a standard of polite and respectful social behavior. She did not allow her love for the kids to spoil them, with the possible exception of

Tía made a decorated birthday cake for every child at the children's home.

the babies. Even the children who were a challenge to love knew that they were valued, as she held them accountable for their actions.

Tía knew how to demonstrate her familial love to the children, and it often happened in the kitchen. Her contribution to the children's lives was like a fountain of love that never ran dry. On the birthday of every child, she would heat up the oven and bake them a decorated cake in the kitchen, which is poorly vented and uncomfortably hot. She used an oven that required that you kneel on the pavers and

One of Tía's handcrafted birthday piñatas

light the pilot light with a match that is attached to a stick by a rubber band, while manipulating the temperature dial. Additionally, she created a birthday piñata of each child's choice and stuffed it with candy. She managed to control the piñata smashing,

and although I could barely stand to watch the chaos, everyone survived the madness.

Tía was the master of multi-tasking and accomplished so much in a way that looked easy. In addition to her many other responsibilities, she managed the medical needs of the children. She was the nurse when the kids were sick or injured. She was knowledgeable about each child's past and current health status. She was the one tasked with taking the children to be examined at the doctor's office or to the hospital when that was necessary. She was not a live-in employee, but she slept at the orphanage when a child needed to be closely monitored throughout the night. She was good at diagnosing medical conditions and looked into the face of blood and guts unflinchingly. She used conventional as well as homeopathic remedies, which once called for a visiting ex-orphan to contribute breast milk to saturate a cotton ball for an earache.

The educational needs of the children were a high priority for Tía. She made sure everyone was prepared for school each weekday, with freshly ironed uniforms and backpacks placed neatly in a row near the front door. The children attended a school that was on the orphanage property, and Tía made sure that snacks were prepared and delivered on time for recess. At the lunchtime break, the most substantial meal of the day was always waiting for the children as well as their teachers. She held the children accountable for completing homework, and when the children needed help with schoolwork, she was their tutor.

Uniforms are a requirement for schools on the island. Some poor children do not attend school because their parents cannot afford uniforms. That was not a problem for anyone under Tía's care. Prior to every new school year, she was busy on the sewing machine and made each student two sets of uniforms. They fit perfectly and looked professionally made. On Roatán, the fifteenth birthday for girls is an important and often elaborate celebration. Can you guess who would sew all the formal attire for the party, which is called a quinceañera?

Tía was also an athlete. Once I talked someone into allowing us to borrow a stand-up paddleboard for our beach day. She never fell off the board, and by the end of the day, she was the stand-up paddleboard champion. Tía was a hands-on guardian for the children, from sports to the culinary arts and everything in between.

This multitalented woman had artistic capabilities on top of everything else. On paper, on chalked sidewalks, on pedicures and manicures, her artwork was impressive. When she first came to the children's home, I noticed that many of the staff and older girls had professional-looking manicures and pedicures. I wondered who was bankrolling all the salon work. I found out that Tía had done everyone's nails! She was also a capable hairstylist and used her skill to make the little girls look loved and well-groomed. She encouraged and taught the children to be creative with pencils, crayons, and any other media at her disposal. She was especially good at helping the boys and girls write letters of appreciation to their sponsors, complete with artwork.

One year, we brought fifty pounds of donated LEGO bricks to the children. They were thrilled to have a toy they had only seen on TV. It was delightful to see their joy, as the children dived into the huge duffle bag of LEGO bricks! You can probably guess who deserved the architectural-designer award for her replica of an ostentatious residence, complete with a flower garden and elaborate swimming pool!

Queen Tía reading a letter of appreciation from one of her beloved children

Pampering Tía with a fan, a cool drink, ice cream, and elevated feet

The defining quality about Tía was that she was completely trustworthy with the children's hearts as well as the resources donated for their physical well-being. In a culture of corruption, where resources are often stolen by unscrupulous leaders, she stood out as an honest steward of contributions that were given and intended for the benefit of the children. She was creative and wise with the limited resources at her disposal.

She once had $500 in US dollars exchanged for me at the best available rate. I would have trusted her with much more than that. If you needed her to shop for you, she would make the purchase and give it to you with the receipt for reimbursement. If you needed something that was available on-site in one of the many cabinets, closets, storage rooms, or the garden, her unique organizational skills guided her to the correct "haystack" to fetch it.

Every June, we had an anniversary celebration to honor Tía for her unreserved love and service. We made her the queen for the day. A golden crown was placed on her head, her feet were elevated, and we attempted to divide and accomplish her daily workload. Everyone wrote her a note of gratitude. One at a time, each child would stand beside their beloved mum and tell her the one thing they loved best about Tía in front of the adoring audience of her little flock. We would finish off the ceremony with a gift presentation and also enjoy a special dessert.

Tía was the "Emmanuel" representative at the children's home, with her hands-on, physical presence. She was a wellspring of the

She wasn't always easy on the kids, but she was a godly example of a mother, and she knew how to spread the love around to all the children. She walked the walk of faith, practicing the pure religion of full-time devotion to orphans.

love and admonition of the Lord. She was wise and full of love, joy, peace, patience, kindness, goodness, faithfulness, gentleness, and self-control. When the kids needed confidence, she shored them up, and when they needed to be humbled, they found that out from Tía. She wasn't always easy on the kids, but she was a godly example of a mother, and she knew how to spread the love around to all the children. She walked the walk of faith, practicing the pure religion of full-time devotion to orphans.

Tía is a Renaissance woman. She is Mother Teresa, Sandra Day O'Connor, Florence Nightingale, and Martha Stewart combined, with a smidge of Lucille Ball added for fun and laughter. When the children needed stability, she was the Rock of Gibraltar. When they needed to be touched by Jesus, she was His flesh-and-bones servant, sent to minister to the orphans. That's why they called her Tía.

RUMINATIONS

I have never met anyone quite as gifted and energetic as Tía. Her sincere faith turned a difficult job into a spectacular ministry.

In a culture of scarcity, where there is an understandable tendency to steal and hoard, Tía was giving and generous. She poured out her life to orphan children who had nothing to give in return.

Tía was loved and admired but sometimes taken for granted. After the writing of this chapter was completed, she was forced to leave her cherished job at the orphanage in order to care for her dying father on the Honduran mainland.

Conventional wisdom says that we are all replaceable, but perhaps Tía is the rare exception. I can tell you that many little hearts were broken with the loss of the woman who functioned as a mother to so many little souls.

The remaining staff she left behind is still scrambling to absorb Tía's responsibilities. They are discovering that the depth and width of Tía's workload was greater than anyone gave her credit for. It will take several workers to replace her, but no one will ever take her place in the hearts of the children.

Certainly, everyone at the orphanage greatly misses Tía and hopes she will someday return to them. She left behind a beautiful legacy of integrity, faith, and love. When she meets her Maker, she will hear the beautiful words, "Well done, good and faithful servant" (Matthew 25:23)!

1. How can you turn your job into a ministry?

2. Describe how you have given to those who had nothing to give in return.

3. What do you want your legacy to be?

TWELVE

SPAGHETTI AND REPENTANCE

*Therefore if any man be in Christ, he is a new creature: old
things are passed away; behold, all things are become new.*
(2 Corinthians 5:17 KJV)

*I*t was difficult to identify Jaime as an image bearer of God
because his behavior was so...well, hellish. I asked someone
who cared for him during his first three years of life for help understanding the boy's unruly behavior. She said, "Oh...Jaime has always
been like that."

From an early age, Jaime frustrated the adults in his life because
of his oppositional behavior. Aside from his strong resistance to
adult supervision, he had no apparent mental or physical disorders.
He disappointed or angered everyone who thought they could convince him to comply with adult authority. When everything went
his way, Jaime could be pleasant. But if things did not go his way,
everyone around him paid a price.

Jaime was a newborn when he was brought to the American-owned orphanage on the island. His tiny body was covered
with scabies. He was affectionately nursed back to health by the
sweet housemother, who treated him like he was her own.

Jaime was one of the few children at the home who fit the dic-
tionary definition of an orphan. His mother was deceased, and his

father was unknown. He never knew what it was like to be part of a typical family. He never witnessed the trauma of abandonment by his biological parents.

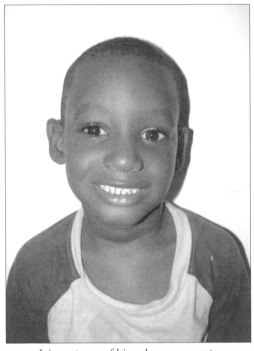
Jaime at one of his calmer moments

The orphanage house-parents who took him in gave him more than his fair share of love and attention. The couple had no children from their union. Jaime was their newborn baby-love. People said that Jaime was the housefather's favorite child, and some observers thought the houseparents even spoiled him.

However, Jaime's houseparents had to leave abruptly. When they left, all the children became orphans once again, but it was especially hard on Jaime. He slept in the nursery, with only a door separating him from the master bedroom of his doting houseparents. He and a little girl named Serena were the favorites and had been absorbed into the nuclear family of the houseparents. The couple had begun the process of adoption for the girl and took her with them when they returned to the United States. However, they left Jaime behind. He was about three years old when he became disconnected from what had been his nuclear family. He would never again be raised by guardians who would treat him like a beloved son.

There was a short interval of time before the interim housepar-ents arrived. Jaime and the other children had to leave the place they called home and were taken temporarily to the Calvary Chapel Son Rise Mission Inn. The kind American missionaries took all of them in and put them to bed at night in various hotel rooms for safekeeping until the new houseparents arrived.

Enter the psychotherapist and her husband. These new temporary houseparents had not been married very long. They didn't have children of their own, so they were short on real-life experience. Her diagnosis of the problem with all the children was that they had been both spoiled and abused. It sounded like an odd judgment, but the original houseparents *had been* different in their approach to parenting. The wife was nurturing; the husband was authoritarian. Jaime's close relationship with the original houseparents put him close to conflicting sources of influence.

The kind psychotherapist made it a habit to tuck little Jaime into bed at night. However, that comforting routine was suddenly stopped when the housemother developed problems in the first trimester of her pregnancy. She was hunkering down in her bedroom trying to manage nausea. As a result, Jaime

Jaime liked doing things differently from the other children.

would never again benefit from the tenderness of being routinely tucked into bed at night by someone who loved him.

The psychotherapist was reluctant to tell any of the children that she was expecting a child, because she thought it would add to the sorrow of her departure. The father-to-be was shouldering the major responsibility of managing the household of out-of-control children. He was overwhelmed. Jaime alone would have overwhelmed anyone.

When I showed up at the orphanage with prenatal pills for the housemother, Jaime was on a time-out in the nursery. I could hear his loud screaming from the upstairs bedroom window. Jaime was aggressive with the other children, and when they retaliated, Jaime would howl with anger. When an adult attempted to resolve the matter, Jaime would take off running like the wind. The adult would have to figure out how to grab the child, carry him upstairs, and then confine him to his room. Jaime would not stay in his room unless the door was locked. The time-out strategy was nonproductive, but it gave the adults a break from the unsustainable effort of trying to control Jaime's unacceptable behavior.

> *I knew how to manage a classroom of thirty-one kindergartners, so I thought I should be able to rein in the child's unpleasant behavior. I exhausted myself trying to do so.*

I knew how to manage a classroom of thirty-one kindergartners, so I thought I should be able to rein in the child's unpleasant behavior. I exhausted myself trying to do so. It was difficult to reason with Jaime. He appeared to enjoy stirring up drama and then being chased by an adult, who would scoop him up in their arms and put him in solitary confinement.

The housefather asked me to drive Jaime to preschool. Jaime liked preschool, so he was happy to climb into the van to go to class. Preschool was only a half day, but it wore him down a bit. When I picked him up from school, I could tell Jaime was not their

Eating ice cream at preschool

favorite student. I was able to coax him back into the van after class with the promise of lunch. It took a lot of energy for Jaime to control his world and everyone in it, so he was an eating machine.

Once, when I was putting Jaime to bed, he was in an unusually cooperative mood. I was helping him put on his pajamas, when I saw a giant cockroach running along the mopboard behind him. I knew Jaime did not like cockroaches, so I kept turning him so his back was toward the crawling cockroach to prevent him from seeing it. But despite my best efforts, Jaime saw the cockroach.

When the other kids heard the screaming, they ran to watch their favorite form of entertainment, which was Jaime's tantrums. An older boy named Nelson decided to save the day. He grabbed a shoe, stood on a chair, and threw the shoe at the cockroach, which had scurried about fourteen feet up the high nursery wall. Nelson nailed it on his first throw, with everyone watching his precision assault on the enemy. We all cheered wildly until we realized that the cockroach had flown from the wall to Nelson's neck! Who knew cockroaches sought revenge, and who knew who would be next? Now *everyone* was screaming, as Nelson was violently swatting the cockroach away from his neck and then finally managed to stomp on the hideous creature with a triumphant crunch, as body armor and guts crunched underfoot.

Nelson was now our favorite superhero. We would enjoy retelling the story for years to come about Nelson the warrior, who had slain the cockroach monster and saved little Jaime. Nelson helped me tuck Jaime into bed. We sang. We prayed. We hugged. We said good night, and all was well in the nursery.

The interim houseparents stayed less than a year. They loved Jaime and gave him tender care and attention, but neither one of them knew what to do about his unacceptable behavior. They tried to resolve Jaime's behavioral issues with all of the psychotherapist's well-intentioned methodologies. Their sincere efforts did little to improve Jaime's non-compliant behavior. When the expectant houseparents said farewell, Jaime and the other children were sad to lose another mother and father figure who told them they were loved but then forever vanished from their lives.

The replacement parents knew exactly how to inspire obedience, and everyone fell into line quickly, with the exception of you-know-who. Every new houseparent gave Jaime less love and attention than the one before, and Jaime treated each new change with more opposition.

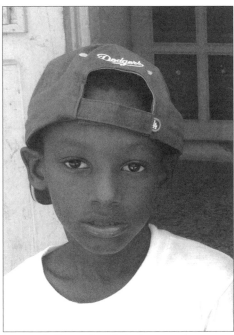

Baseball caps for all the boys, and Jaime picked the best team in the league!

Jaime was an unlovable child before the newest houseparents arrived, but he became all the more so as the tenderness of being tucked into bed at night and other forms of nurturing diminished. A harsh and comprehensive discipline strategy was put into place, which was not balanced with any sort of love or affirmation of his value as an image-bearer of God. Jaime didn't like the change and was placed on time-outs more than ever. After being isolated in his room, Jaime would scream, kick the door, and throw things. Jaime started living in his room for an inordinate amount of time. You could hear him screaming for hours, even though his howling did not give him a good return for his effort.

Jaime missed out on every fun activity at the children's home, sometimes watching the fun play out before him in the courtyard or baseball field that was beneath his upstairs bedroom window. After a while, Jaime's frequent screaming became normalized, and everyone carried on with activities as if there were no sound coming from Jaime's room.

Once, I witnessed a man pick up little Jaime to show him some love. Although the man had spent a lot of time with the child and proven himself to be gentle and kindhearted, Jaime struck a significant blow to the man's head. I overheard some adults who were worried that Jaime would grow up and go to jail.

When Jaime started elementary school, he did not conform to the new school program like the other students, even though his teachers used corporal punishment. Jaime spent a lot of time in the principal's office, and there were frequent conferences and notes sent home to his houseparents.

Jaime's behavior wore on everyone at the home. The desire to continue caring for the boy was understandably weak. When Jaime was eight years old, there was an unexpected turn of events that would forever change the course of his life. The narrative for the sudden change was that a Roatán couple had come to the children's home looking to adopt a boy. They chose the one who spent most of his time confined to his bedroom because he made everyone's life miserable with his loud and defiant behavior. There were two other boys at the home who were much more pleasant and almost the same age. According to the story, the couple received permission to take Jaime home with them prior to formal adoption procedures. If all this had been true, it would have been Jaime's golden opportunity. However, allegedly, the couple decided against adopting him after having him in their home for only a matter of days. The whole account lacked credibility. However, it served to rationalize the administrative decision that followed, which must have been the most traumatic event in Jaime's young life. It was decided that Jaime could no longer live at the only home he had lived in for the first eight years of his life. Jaime's expulsion was one of seven cases that I knew about at the orphanage. Failure to comply at the home was a one-way ticket to another institution that was guaranteed to be less comfortable.

Jaime was placed at the Honduran-owned orphanage on Roatán, which was for boys only. It was not nearly as well funded as his first home. Jaime was suddenly immersed in the culture of poverty at the poorly maintained children's home on the other side of the island. The cruise-ship visitors bringing goodies and fried chicken from Bojangles rarely visited his new orphanage because it wasn't a pretty sight.

At the end of the first year that Jaime was transferred to his new residence, the boys and girls from his previous orphanage came to visit on Christmas Day. They showed up to hand over their surplus unwanted gifts to the poor children at the Honduran-owned orphanage. Jaime was thrilled to see all the familiar faces. He wept bitterly when they left and begged to go home with them.

The new orphanage did not have a dedicated room or the manpower to manage Jaime's behavior. There were older boys that were rough on Jaime when he bothered them. He was probably beaten up a lot. I visited him annually on his birthday to keep tabs on him. His behavior improved but continued to be unacceptable.

Jaime was no one's favorite at the second orphanage. Besides being aggressive and loud, he did not fail to spread his unique form of love to those in authority. Jaime had to answer to a woman named Bella, the live-in caregiver to the twelve boys at the home. Bella was not a soft touch. She told me a story that perfectly illustrates Jaime's modus operandi. It was a scene made for Hollywood. Bella had just washed and line dried all the white clothes for the boys. Imagine how Bella had carefully laid out the folded and sorted laundry on a long rectangular table for the boys to pick up and take to their rooms after eating the spaghetti dinner she had prepared for them. Can you tell where this story is going? Now imagine Jaime taking a full plate of spaghetti and carefully aiming and sliding his dinner off the plate with the intent of soiling all the freshly laundered clothing! Bella had a strong reaction to the incident and boasted about winning the battle with her harsh punishment. I don't know why I thought Jaime's spaghetti trick was a bit funny, but I kept a straight face during her retelling of the drama. The episode was one of those unforgettable moments with Jaime's name written all over it.

At nine years of age, Jaime was a nonreader—not that he was incapable of learning to read, but because his behavior made him learning resistant. On one of my assignments to the island, Jaime allowed me to teach him some basic reading and writing skills in just a few weeks. It was not a difficult task because Jaime was willing to learn, and he was developmentally mature enough to catch on quickly. I always knew he was smart—just naughty.

Because I have always loved this bad boy, I offered to pay the tuition for Jaime's private Christian-school education. It's cheap compared to U.S. private schools. This was a golden opportunity for Jaime because the government schools in Honduras are not good. After a year and a half, Jaime hit his teacher and was expelled from the school. They don't have continuous enrollment in Honduran public schools, so he missed out on half the school year and instead stayed home with Bella. I'm sure they made one another's lives miserable. I was thinking about giving up on the kid.

Sometimes I think back to those frustrated adults at the first orphanage who worried that Jaime was going to grow up and go to jail. When I originally wrote this chapter of the book, I wondered if I should delete it, because Jaime was not a success story. The chapter was mostly an explanation of all the sad reasons why Jaime might actually grow up and go to jail.

As it turned out, Jaime almost did go to jail. But God sent Jaime and the other boys a pastor to disciple them in the faith. The man set up an office at the home and slept on a mattress on the floor once a week so he could love and nurture the boys and encourage them to live out the Christian faith. The man and his wife had three small studio apartments attached to their home that the man's father had built for his own children. The good pastor and his wife used the apartments as a halfway house to shelter the boys when they transitioned from the orphanage to independent living.

The pastor encouraged the boys to think of one another as brothers who belonged to a big family. He had family photos taken of the boys with their caregivers and decorated the living room with the framed pictures. Every holiday, the pastor and his lovely wife prepared a festive meal and also made sure the boys all had a special gift on Christmas Day. The pastor was born and raised on the island and had a good reputation, unlike others associated with the home. To add to his résumé, the pastor had exceptional culinary skills and baked fresh bread for the boys!

During Jaime's teenage years, there was a problematic "brother" at the orphanage named Virgil who was far worse than Jaime, but Virgil knew how to keep his bad behavior under the radar. Jaime's "brother" Virgil was in the habit of sneaking out of the house after dark with a friend who owned a gun. Together, they raised hell. Virgil drew attention to his criminal activity when he held a gun to the head of an influential man's wife. Virgil had distinguishing facial features that made him stand out in a crowd. He was identified as the perpetrator of the crime and has been on the lam since then. The last update about Virgil was that he was using the gun to rob people elsewhere on the island. If and when they find him, he will be arrested and put in jail.

It was discovered that Jaime had sneaked out at night with Virgil on at least one occasion. I'm not sure what lured him out on the streets at night. He grew up in a sheltered environment at his first orphanage and rarely went out after dark. Jaime had an anger-management problem, but he was not an evil child. I'm a little biased, but I believe that Jaime spent his time out with Virgil frightened and hiding in the bushes. However, no one knew for sure if Jaime was involved in the criminal activity with Virgil when he held the gun to the woman's head, so he was taken to the police station for questioning. Before he left home, Jaime's mentor told him to gather up any belongings and snacks that he would want to take with him to jail in the event the police arrested him. In Honduras, they have frightening, no-nonsense jails. Overcrowding, violence, and sexual abuse are commonplace. When Jaime climbed into the truck cab with the only father figure he had ever trusted, he knew there was a possibility that he might not be coming home.

Fortunately, no one recognized Jaime as being an accomplice to the crime with the woman who identified Virgil. He came home with the pastor, who sensed this was a life-defining moment. Together, they talked, they cried, and they prayed. The preacher told him he needed to decide if he wanted to be a good person or a criminal. After almost sixteen years of being the infamous bad boy at two orphanages, Jaime made a monumental decision. He decided he wanted to be a good person.

The change in Jaime's life was a good example of Biblical repentance. We all need to make the all-important decision to believe in Jesus and repent, but deep and sincere repentance tends to lag behind believing. However, without much delay, Jaime's repentance resulted in a tectonic shift in behavior and a welcome relief to those who were in authority over him. As a small child, he was a screamer. Later, his behavior screamed of defiance to anyone who thought they could control the kid—especially if spaghetti was on the menu. However, when I saw Jaime three months after his decision to repent, he was cooperating with the spaghetti chef, quietly and diligently cleaning all the glass window slats in the front of the home, just as she had told him to do. It was none too soon for him to rein in his rebellious behavior, because by then Jaime was six feet tall and towered over the spaghetti chef. As I watched Jaime cleaning the windows, I silently delighted in the thought, "He's not going to jail after all!" He was a living, breathing, tall miracle.

Jaime's behavioral shift created a small problem for me. I had already written this chapter about his life, but Jaime had done an about-face, and his life story was being providentially rewritten. It was a joy to visit my tall friend after the trip to the police station that redefined Jaime's life. Among the first words he spoke to me were, "I want to be a good person." I stopped our small-group English class and asked him to explain himself because it was out of character for him to talk like that. He didn't have a very good explanation, even though I tried to pull one out of him. He may have been embarrassed about filling me in on the details of his after-dark escapades, which I learned about at a later time.

It was as if someone had flipped a switch in Jaime's behavior. The two of us had some meaningful conversations about our history together since he was three years old. I showed him several photos on my phone that I had taken of him throughout his childhood. I had one of him smiling and holding a small whiteboard from when he had learned to read and write for the first time. I told him I had more photos at home on my computer. Throughout the years, God had used me like a slender recurring thread woven into the tapestry of Jaime's life, and then God gave me the privilege of standing back to see His beautiful handiwork.

Jaime learns to read!

My annual Great Commission assignments on the island fell during Jaime's birthday month. I had taken him small gifts throughout the years for his birthday, but this year I was taking him the gift of his dreams. The timing of the gift was perfect because of the miraculous change that had happened to Jaime, which can only be described as divine intervention.

Before I left for Roatán, my eldest son and his wife surprised me by donating used iPhones for the older boys at the orphanage. The boys received the phones with great enthusiasm—no matter that they were used phones. I videotaped them thanking my son and his wife for their kindness. In one of the videos, an eighteen-year-old named Geraldo choked up with emotion and could barely hold back tears of joy.

The phones were given out according to age and merit. I was surprised when the pastor messaged me before I left for the island to say that I could bring a phone for Jaime. I didn't learn until after I arrived that Jaime had repented of his bad behavior. I was thrilled to give the phone to him a few days before his sixteenth birthday. He used the phone to message me before I left the island. He called me Mom. It made me cry.

RUMINATIONS

Disrespectful and disobedient children are usually not my favorite kids. However, there was something about Jaime that I loved from the start. That love was probably sustainable because I only experienced him in small doses. Plus, I came to the orphanage bearing gifts and offering engaging child-centered activities. I always began with a discussion about behavioral expectations and an incentive program with rewards for good behavior. Jaime wanted the goodies.

After our five-year relationship, from Jaime's third to his eighth year of life, he was transferred to the orphanage on the other side of the island. From then on, my interaction with him was limited. Most years, I only saw him once, and sometimes he only seemed interested in the birthday gift I brought him. However, there was a connection between the two of us because I was a small but nevertheless persistent presence in Jaime's life, which I documented with photos for his future reference.

> *Persistence paid off. Jaime knows that he is special to me. Love never does fail.*

It was thrilling to see how God used a crisis coupled with the guidance of a godly mentor to transform Jaime's life. Although my interaction with Jaime has been minimal for the second half of his life, persistence paid off. Jaime knows that he is special to me. Love never does fail. I haven't invested enough of myself to deserve being called his mom, but I'll take it.

1. What is the Biblical definition of *repentance*?

2. Read Matthew 28:16–20. Why did Jesus make discipleship an important component of the Great Commission?

3. What is the significance of one person (like the good pastor in Jaime's life) who loves and disciples another person in the faith?

4. Long-term relationships with unlovable people are difficult to sustain. Describe a rewarding outcome of persistent love from your life experience.

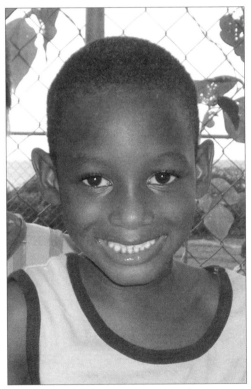

My last photo of Jaime at the
Sandy Bay Orphanage

THIRTEEN

DEATH, BETRAYAL,
AND THE CANCER CONNECTION

*She is clothed with strength and dignity, and she laughs without fear
of the future.* (Proverbs 31:25 NLT)

It was the worst year of my life. First came the horror of my breast-cancer diagnosis and then the agonizing weeks that followed, with so many unknowns.

My plans for a family reunion in Yosemite were ruined because I was scheduled for radiation at the same time we had reserved in the national park to vacation with my children and grandchildren.

After the removal of the tumor, my surgeon told me that my prognosis was good and that the pathologist was not suggesting chemotherapy. This was a wonderful relief until I went to the hematology oncologist, who told me that chemotherapy was still on the table until genomic testing of the tumor was completed. It took weeks before the report came back, and thankfully, it was decided that the side effects from chemotherapy outweighed the benefits. Cancer is a scary rollercoaster ride, followed by surveillance and unpleasant procedures that never seem to go away.

Ten days after my surgery, the shock of my diagnosis became of secondary importance when one of my adult children had a life crisis that almost destroyed him. It shook my soul.

Around the same time, I fell outdoors, which resulted in a blunt-force head injury that sent me to the emergency room. It was a minor injury that didn't require stitches, and there was no concussion. However, blood vessels had ruptured from the impact, and the internal bleeding made my forehead swell until I looked like an alien from outer space. The swelling went down rather quickly, but the popped blood vessels resulted in shades of bright pink and purple bruising on my forehead. The bright colors traveled slowly down my face from my forehead to under my chin, lingering in the area underneath my lower eyelids. I looked frightful for more than a month.

I hid from the world until the bruising went away and prayed myself through an avalanche of heartache and fear. My world was turned upside down, and for several months I lived on the edge of anxiety and panic. I used stage makeup on my face to cover up the bruising when I had to go out for twenty-six radiation treatments. I became depressed and cried every day, hoping that I would cry less with each passing day. I never thought anything good would ever come of my pathetic situation.

It added to my sorrow to notify the director at the orphanage on Roatán that I would not be coming with a team that year because of my treatments and recovery. I wondered if I would ever return to the orphanage.

When I mentioned the dates and job description to my surgeon, I was surprised to hear her tell me that there was no reason not to go!

The timeframe for the work at the orphanage "just happened" to be delayed three months later than usual that year, but it still seemed unlikely that there would be enough time for me to recover from cancer treatments and show up for the assignment. However, when I mentioned the dates and job description to my surgeon, I was surprised to hear her tell me that there was no reason not to go!

I wanted to contact the director immediately to tell him I would be able to work at the orphanage after all, but I didn't have a team and I couldn't do the job alone. Shortly after that, I received an unsolicited phone call from a friend of a friend who had previously worked at the orphanage. She wanted to know if my next mission trip would be at a time that would fit into her busy and complicated schedule. I gave her the dates when the director needed to take a leave of absence. The dates fit into her schedule perfectly. She said she had several friends who wanted to tag along. They turned out to be a dream team.

Our team went in the fall to accommodate the director's trip to the United States for an orphanage board meeting. While we were on assignment, social services surprised us with three small children. One of them was a four-month-old baby boy whose name was unknown. I was concerned about

Tía with the dream team

the additional burden of a baby because babies require so much time and attention, but the women on the team were delighted to have a baby to care for. They were known as the baby whisperers at their church. I handed little Mr. No Name over to them for safekeeping, thinking God was a whole lot better at picking teams than me.

The baby whisperers freed me up to interact with the other children and staff members. Giana was a fourteen-year-old who was comfortable in the company of adults and liked to be in the kitchen helping with meal preparation. Some of our best times had been in the kitchen, where we turned hard work in a hot kitchen into fun and laughter.

The baby whisperers enjoyed caring for the little ones.

Giana had always held a special place in my heart. I loved her the minute I met her when she was only ten years old. She was a bundle of cuteness with a sweet personality. Giana was talkative, but she did not talk about where she came from or the circumstances that had landed her at the orphanage. Some of the children at the orphanage talk freely about their lives prior to living at the group home. Others never do.

Giana and I enjoyed spending time together, but after knowing one another for four years, we were about to develop a special new bond. I had nearly completed my assignment at the home when Giana indicated that we needed to talk. She waited until my last night to open up a discussion about something that most girls her age don't talk about. I was making my nightly rounds to say goodnight and tuck everyone into bed. When I came to Giana's bedroom, she was a bit nervous as she initiated the conversation.

"Miss Rebecca, are you sick?" she asked.

"Of course not, Giana! Do I look sick?" I responded without knowing where the discussion was going.

Giana told me that she had overheard adults saying I would not be coming to the orphanage that year because I had breast

> *Giana had survived a level of loss and betrayal that was so suffocating it must have been hard for her to breathe while it was happening.*

cancer. I was glad to be able to honestly tell Giana that I had a good prognosis and it looked like I would be around for a while. Then the discussion became less about me and more about how cancer had rattled Giana's young life. We had shared meaningful times of companionship before, but Giana had never come close to sharing about her heartbreaking former life.

Giana had survived a level of loss and betrayal that was so suffocating it must have been hard for her to breathe while it was happening. She poured out her heart and explained how cancer had robbed her of her early childhood. How devastating it must have been for a little girl to watch her beloved mommy slowly die of cancer, especially without access to adequate medical care.

Giana's heartache was multiplied by later trauma inflicted upon her by her father. He appeared at first to be a hero when he showed up to take responsibility for his two daughters after their mother died. He turned out to be a dark villain instead. Giana was not believed when she first spoke up about his sexual abuse. Eventually, she and her younger sister were rescued from the abhorrent situation and placed at the orphanage. Giana lost her mother to cancer and her father to evil.

The sharing of our experiences with cancer knit our hearts together. As it turned out, my cancer diagnosis was a portal for Giana to open up and enter into a safe place where she felt heard and understood. My history with cancer became a way for Giana to release some of her residual pain and sorrow. I think she put off our heart-to-heart talk until my last night because it took courage to unpack old memories of death and sexual abuse. I already knew in my head that there was a purpose for trials and that God does not waste our suffering. It was affirming to experience that firsthand.

I was astonished at Giana's resiliency after surviving two catastrophic events prior to her tenth birthday. Either one in isolation might have negatively impacted her ability to live a happy, well-balanced life, especially without a single adult family member to lead her out of the dark storm and into a future of recovery.

Giana must have been comforted by the safety and stability of the children's home when she first arrived as a broken little girl. She immediately bonded with the remarkable woman who was the primary caretaker for the children and also the heart of the home. Giana spent the majority of her discretionary time in the kitchen with Tía, who became her second mother. It only took one beautiful and loving soul to make the difference between wholeness and brokenness.

God used Tía's love and mentoring to enable Giana to become more than a survivor. Tía was a problem solver and took the initiative when action needed to be taken. She showed Giana how to do the same. Tía lovingly discipled Giana in the faith and also modeled the dignity and reward of hard work.

No one would ever guess Giana had suffered from childhood trauma. She is happy and has an engaging sense of humor. She is confident and compassionate. She is one of those intelligent and versatile individuals who can adapt to almost any setting, from a preschool play center to the presidential palace. Her executive skills make her a natural leader that others want to follow. Most important, she is a young woman of faith.

After finishing high school, Giana was accepted into a nursing program at a university on the mainland. I'm hoping she figures out that medical school would be a better fit for her, and I believe she will. Perhaps she will someday be an oncologist.

Giana laughs often. She refuses to allow the past to rob her of joyfully and fearlessly living out her future. She reminds me of the lady of Proverbs 31, who "is clothed with strength and dignity, and she laughs without fear of the future" (Proverbs 31:25 NLT).

RUMINATIONS

Giana is a rare example of a success story at the orphanage. Unlike all the others, she has left the home to study at a university, but that is not the most important part of her story. She is different from the other orphans, who drift away with the strong current of the island culture instead of living out the Christian faith. The girls usually leave between the ages of sixteen and twenty and soon become pregnant, without the benefit of marriage. The boys move out of the orphanage to move in with a girlfriend or for worse reasons, sometimes—regrettably—resulting from bad experiences at the orphanage.

Giana's close personal relationship with an adult mentor who loved her enough to teach her the Biblical alternative to the island culture set her apart from all the others. Every child at the home was sheltered, fed, clothed, and sent to school. Giana received so much more than that.

Her faith in God delivered her from the sorrowful events of her childhood, and you would never guess that she was seriously traumatized as a child. She has excellent social skills and a Biblical work ethic. She has had the unique advantage of walking through the second half of her life with someone who modeled these commendable character traits.

Giana stumbled onto that opportunity for discipleship because of her brokenness. She clung to Tía's apron strings from the day she arrived at the children's home because she needed the life support of someone who was willing to love her without disappointing her.

Giana was discipled according to Deuteronomy 6:7, mostly in the kitchen. While she was attached to Tía's hip, she was informally taught Biblical precepts as they went from task to task. Faith took hold in Giana's heart because Tía practiced what she preached as they walked through life together. Tía's job was not to disciple Giana or any of the children, but it happened organically because of Giana's original emotional dependence upon her adopted auntie. The orphanage leadership in the United States has worked selflessly on behalf of the children, but they don't seem to understand the critical importance of discipling them to produce true followers of Jesus. They have repeated the same mistake as the church in Honduras, and the outcome has been disastrous for the children when they transition to independent living.

That same leadership has overperformed in various projects, like a fish farm, fruit and vegetable gardens, chicken farming, the founding of an on-campus school for the orphans that is open to children in the community, plus ambitious building projects that never end. They have also engaged in ministries beyond the orphanage, like feeding the hungry, building homes for the poor, and delivering Christmas gifts to underprivileged children. They have made the mistake of majoring in peripheral things and missing out on the main thing.

Fortunately, Giana's brokenness put her in a position to be discipled. The child was so needy when she first arrived that it must have been draining for Tía. To her credit, Tía seized the ministry opportunity and gave the girl a gift that will last for all eternity. It is noteworthy that Tía also went through a cancer scare, but the tumor turned out to be benign. That must have been an even bigger scare for Giana.

Giana and I liked each other from the beginning. We became close through the time-honored tradition of tucking children into bed. I often saved Giana for last so I didn't have to hurry to the next child before they fell asleep. She was a delight to my soul, and I enjoyed our evening chats and prayer time. She has a lovely singing voice, so *she* would sing our bedtime love song to me and her younger sister.

On that final night when she asked about my cancer, I was glad to tell her that my chances of survival were excellent. That is when she poured out her heart about her childhood trauma. My bout with cancer clearly resonated with Giana. Shared experiences of suffering are healing to the soul.

It was an excellent thing that Giana was "accidentally" discipled by Tía, who probably did not have time for something extra that was not part of her job description. I don't know of another child who has left the orphanage with the Christian faith in their heart and a Biblical worldview in their head.

Because Tía taught Giana everything she knew about the faith, God had an opening in Giana's heart to raise up beauty from the ashes of her life and set her up as a success story.

1. How would you define a life success story from a Biblical perspective?

2. Read Deuteronomy 6:7 and think about the nuts and bolts of Biblical discipleship.

3. Have you ever majored in the minor things in life and missed out on the things of eternal value?

4. How has God used your suffering to mature you in the faith and prepare you to reach out to others?

FOURTEEN

VARMINT ENCOUNTERS OF THE WORST KIND

Have I not commanded you? Be strong and courageous! Do not be terrified or dismayed (intimidated), for the LORD your God is with you wherever you go. (Joshua 1:9)

WARNING: Some people may be bothered by the descriptions of the following encounters with unpleasant animals in Central America.

*U*nwanted experiences with troublesome animals have been an unavoidable and significant part of my Great Commission adventures. The humid, tropical climate of Central America makes the region rich with creature encounters of the worst kind. I have not enjoyed the bedbugs, bats, botflies, and biting dogs, but they have added something unique to my travels. Of course, I have only appreciated those experiences in retrospect as memories of adventure and survival.

I marveled at Joy Dellinger's story about stepping out of her car in Belize to bravely soak in a wild encounter with a jaguar off in the distance. Some women like to mix their faith with adventure; Joy could have written a book about this. It would have been an incredible read, because Joy understood the true purpose and value of the Great Commission, and no amount of varmints could have restrained her from going forth to any distant place where God led her. Nothing mattered to her as much as the Great Commission.

I still haven't untangled my irrational fear of cockroaches, which was developed in Joy and N. T. Dellinger's house when I was awakened by a large one nesting in my hair. Using the bathroom at the Dellinger home after dark forced the difficult decision: do I turn on the lights and attract the wasp-type insects that come out of the seams of the wood paneling, or do I leave the lights off and allow cockroaches to crawl around underfoot?

The Dellingers seemed unfazed by the insects, wildcats, hopping mice, and even the fer-de-lance, known to scientists as the Bothrops asper and to the natives as the "jumping tommygoff." It is a pit snake dreaded by locals, and its bite can lead to infection, amputation, and even death. Although it can grow to six feet long, the specimen I saw marinating in a jar of formaldehyde at a national park was only about two feet long. These dreaded snakes are a part of the local folklore, which embellishes their characteristics as aggressive, jumping vipers that pursue their victims beneath the jungle canopy. One local's rendition of the fer-de-lance folklore described how they pretend to flee at first and then turn and mercilessly chase down their victim in order to sink their fangs into human flesh!

The dreaded fer-de-lance

I asked the park ranger if it was safe to walk alone in the jungle when I visited St. Herman's Blue Hole National Park in the interior of Belize. The place is known throughout Latin America for its beautiful sapphire water that fills a sinkhole that was once a cave. The ranger assured me that it was not a problem, and he gave me the old and questionable story about snakes being more afraid of humans than vice versa. He told me that snakebites usually happen when snakes enter homes or because they are difficult to see and, therefore, people come too close to them. He gave me a mini lecture about the bad people who kill the fer-de-lance snake, all of whom should leave the poor creature alone.

His only warning was for me to watch where I was stepping, because if the snake thought I was going to stomp on it, it could bite. So, I was looking very carefully at where I placed my feet as I walked through the soggy jungle. I was covered in protective gear from head to toe to mitigate against mosquitos because I was concerned about malaria and dengue fever. I tied my umbrella to my belt loop, along with a plastic grocery bag to hold some of my gear so my hands would be free in case I slipped. St. Herman's cave was both eerie and magnificent, but I kept my distance from the edge of the water because there was no protective railing to prevent people from sliding down its slippery slope.

> *I was halfway up the steps when I noticed the blur of a snake quickly moving underfoot just as I was about to set my foot down on the damp earth.*

Being alone brings out my true cowardice. I decided to take an ascending path on wood-framed dirt stairs that I hoped would lead me to higher and drier ground. I was halfway up the steps when I noticed the blur of a snake quickly moving underfoot just as I was about to set my foot down on the damp earth. I had been primed to panic because of the snake stories I had heard about the deadly fer-de-lance. So, right on cue, I did a 180-degree turn and began my sprint back to the ranger station, hoping I wouldn't slip as I descended the earthen stairs.

I made it to the bottom of the stairs and began running through the muddy jungle path with my heart pounding out of my chest. I had not seen another soul on my hike and feared that I would be found dead from a heart attack, lying on the jungle floor, half-eaten by a jaguar or perhaps nibbled upon by the carnivorous ants that eat small birds in the rainforests of Belize. Worst of all, I could clearly hear the fer-de-lance chasing me through the dense rainforest!

Or so I thought. I was halfway back to the ranger station, out of breath and energy, when I realized that the rustling sound that I heard was not a jumping tommygoff pursuing me. It was the rustling of the plastic grocery bag that I had tied to my belt loop. This snake experience forever changed my fascination with the jungle. I never again hiked the rainforest solo. I do enjoy telling this snake story to my grandchildren. I'm always prepared with a plastic bag in my pocket so I can demonstrate how the rustling of a plastic grocery bag sounds like a snake in pursuit, aggressively slithering on its belly through the flora of the tropical rainforest.

When I returned to the park entrance and told the ranger about the blurry image of the snake I nearly stepped on, he seemed amused at my horror. He told me the snake I described was a nonvenomous type of snake in a species called racers because of their swiftness. He smiled and told me I could have picked it up and played with the reptile. As if normal people who see snakes in the wild pick them up and play with them.

This brings me to the unbelievable but true story of a young man I met on the island of Roatán, who *did* pick up and play with a snake in the wild. It was a deadly coral snake. These snakes are strikingly beautiful because of their brilliant color and diminutive size. They look more like gigantic worms than snakes in size. The coral snake bit the young man while he was handling it, which sent him in pursuit of the nearest source of medical care. He and his missionary friend were told that there was no antivenom on the island, and that once the painful and potentially fatal reaction to the venom begins, it progresses rapidly and is difficult to reverse. The young man and his friend boarded the first available flight back to the United States. He was racked with pain and in a wheelchair before he made it to a medical center where he could be treated with antivenom. After hearing him tell me the story, I couldn't resist asking him why on earth he had picked up the venomous snake. His reply would only have made sense to someone like Steve Irwin the Crocodile Hunter.

One of the dead coral snakes I saw while walking on the island

The endemic species of coral snakes found only on the island of Roatán are considered extremely endangered. That's according to the IUCN website that tracks the snakes, but I saw four of them during my brief habitual power walks on the island. I have photographed and/or reported one live one and three dead ones on the west end of the island. I sent photos of the dead snakes to the Red List Unit of the IUCN. The scientist asked for a photo of the live coral snake, but I ran like an Olympic sprinter when it slid down a steep embankment alongside the road and appeared only a few feet in front of me as I was power walking. The scientists who think coral snakes on Roatán are so rare should start walking around the west end of the island. I stopped walking as a form of exercise because of the snakes (as well as the ferocious dogs that chased me) and opted for the safety of water aerobics instead.

Thankfully, I wasn't present when a teenager at the American-owned orphanage on Roatán killed a boa constrictor, only seven miles from my coral-snake sightings. The boa was underneath the apartments built for visiting missionaries at the children's home. In these same apartments, some poor missionary was bitten by a scorpion in his bed! I usually pull back the sheets and check for scorpions before hopping into bed when I stay in those apartments. The boa constrictor greatly diminished the population of island rats at the orphanage, but it was neutralized out of a concern that the snake might swallow one of the little girls who lived at the home.

At the same orphanage, a vine snake was discovered upstairs in one of the girls' bedrooms. They were terrified until screens were put on the windows to prevent that from happening again.

There was one snake encounter at the orphanage that I remember rather fondly. We were down on the field below the main house. I saw Soledad approaching me with a midsize dead snake that she held by the tail in her outstretched hand. The boys had found it in a tree and beat it to death with sticks. Soledad was cautiously but proudly holding the limp reptile far away from her body. She walked toward me with a smirk on her face and dropped it at my feet, most likely for the shock value and the opportunity to hear me scream like a crazy woman. The kids thought my irrational fear of cockroaches was hysterically funny, and they undoubtedly plotted and hoped that my reaction to the snake would be wildly entertaining. I'm even afraid of dead snakes, but I decided to take a deep breath and remain calm, especially since the snake looked absolutely lifeless. I thought I would show the kids that I could be brave. However, after Soledad dropped the serpent to the ground, it began to slither away! We all screamed and ran away from the scene. Barto, the groundskeeper at the orphanage, was out on the field. He is a hunter and was unfazed by the nearly dead reptile. We all watched as he picked up the snake by the tail, started twirling it above his head like a lasso, and then sent it flying hundreds of feet, high over the fence into the neighbor's yard. Barto instantly turned our panic into relief by rescuing us from the vine snake that appeared to be completely dead but was not dead.

In my personal experience, men tend to be better equipped than women to manage snake encounters. A team member, whom we called MacGyver, came along as a handyman and also functioned as a lifeguard. Not only did he fix every broken thing in sight, but he was prepared to die to protect the boys and girls from a sea snake. We were at the beach for the day, when he calmly but urgently told me there was a sea snake beneath him in the shallow Caribbean water where he and the children were playing. He had spotted the creature and told me he would stay in the water to track its whereabouts and directed me to quickly remove all the children from the water.

The truth of the matter is that there are no sea snakes in the Caribbean, but MacGyver did not know that. I was only aware of this fact because I had previously seen similar "sea snakes" while snorkeling in the area. I also paused in fear the first time I saw one while snorkeling alone, thinking it was a sea snake. That's when I learned that you can scream and snorkel at the same time. After researching the topic on the Internet, I found out that there are no sea snakes in the Caribbean, only snake eels, which are appropriately named because they closely resemble sea snakes and look different than

normal ribbon-shaped eels. Even though there are no sea snakes in the Caribbean, I thought MacGyver handled the situation with great bravery. Most people would have bolted out of the water, screaming for everyone to come ashore.

There *are* rather large moray eels that live close to the shoreline in the

Spotted snake eels are not venemous, but they can bite.

marine park on Roatán. I saw one swimming freely past me in the opposite direction while I was snorkeling through a narrow passage where there was no room for either of us to turn around. It avoided me and I avoided it and we both survived. Eels give me a fright, but not like snakes, which tend to show up in unexpected places, sometimes indoors.

Snakes and rats tend to share the same territory, since snakes are one level above rats on the food chain. Pandy Town, Roatán, is a picturesque town that has a substantial population of island rats because of the abundant food supply that floats on top of the water directly underneath the stilted houses. The people who live there have not been indoctrinated about the evil of littering like those of us who live in the United States, where littering is considered an unforgivable sin. On one of my Great Commission assignments, I stayed in one of the most upscale homes in the area, which was built partly stilted over the water of the bay in Pandy Town. The home was located where most of the floating garbage accumulates. Instead of throwing our watermelon rinds into a trashcan, I watched as the rinds were tossed out of an open window and afterward heard them splash in the Caribbean Sea.

The rats and cockroaches thrive on the garbage that surrounds the stilted homes in Pandy Town.

I almost gasped out loud. I thought my friends back in the United States would never believe me, so I stealthily took photos of the floating garbage when no one was looking. The vast expanse of trash included everything from rotting food to waterlogged lumber.

> *It made me uncomfortable to hear the rats inside the walls while I was trying to fall asleep at night, wondering if they would crawl on me as I slept.*

The big shock in the otherwise-lovely home was the obvious presence of island rats that thrived on the shore-to-shore food supply that was floating underneath the house. You could hear the rats moving inside the walls of the house and you could see the "Tom and Jerry" doorways that they had chewed where the walls intersected with the floor.

It made me uncomfortable to hear the rats inside the walls while I was trying to fall asleep at

There are many beautiful butterflies and moths on the island, but this one on my window at night was creepy.

This tarantula was on the wall outside my room.

Frogs are common on the island, and some of them are loud at night.

Dead bugs on my window sill, including the loud and dreaded cicada

Nocturnal land crabs can be startling when they creep out of their daytime hiding places.

night, wondering if they would crawl on me as I slept. The wildest encounter happened in the bathroom, which was the only room in the house with a door. I was brushing my teeth when I heard rats snarling at each other in the ceiling above me. I looked up and noticed that there was a large opening in the ceiling directly above the sink through which I could see the two rats that were fighting. Suddenly, I had to dodge something that fell from the ceiling into the sink. I screamed loudly, but what I feared was a rat falling from the ceiling was only a piece of wood that the combative rats had dislodged.

At another location at one of the orphanages on the mainland, we put out rat poison after a rat was found nesting in someone's suitcase, plus there were too many sightings for our comfort. Earlier in the day, I was wearing flip-flops when a rat ran across my foot as I walked through the kitchen. After putting out the pink granules of rat poison, I saw a rat that was motionless, located at the edge of the kitchen counter. I assumed the poison had killed it in its tracks. I was alone in the kitchen and decided to be brave and save others from seeing the hideous creature. I grabbed a hand broom and waste pan to remove the rat. However, when I attempted to sweep the rat into the dustpan, it terrified me when it scurried away from sight. Apparently, the creature was not quite dead yet.

If you do mission work in the tropics, you are going to have close encounters with an assortment of varmints. It's nice when you can capture the moment with a photo. I'm still terrified by Central American cockroaches, scorpions, grasshoppers, vicious dogs, and snakes, but I'm warming up to tarantulas, which are the most common roadkill on Roatán. The loud woodpeckers and roosters that wake you up at predawn are also not that bad. The pet monkeys, geckos, frogs, nocturnal land crabs, and iguanas add to the ambiance of the setting and don't bother me, as long as they don't catch me by surprise.

The tropics of Central America are full of varmints in the air, land, and sea. I could go on with more examples of creepy critters, like the microscopic parasites, viruses, and bacteria in the tap water, which are probably a greater threat than larger animal forms. However, I think there is an unspoken taboo about missionaries going on and on about the horrors of varmints, which is why I started this chapter with a warning. It is advisable to frontload Great Commission travel with some knowledge about the types of local varmints at your destination, especially since there are mitigations for minimizing encounters with troublesome creatures.

The tropical rainforests of Central America have given rise to an abundance of wildlife, as well as an ethos that has inspired Hollywood productions that have thrilled moviegoers for decades. Pesky animals are part of the adventure for those missionaries who dare to live in that unique region of the world. Perhaps no other place offers a better opportunity to accumulate a treasure trove of adventure stories to share with the grandkids. Varmints might even be considered an inconvenient benefit of sorts, and there are seasoned missionaries like Joy Dellinger who are capable of stepping out of the momentary apprehension to face wildlife encounters with courage. For the rest of us, I recommend packing spider and rat traps and paying your host to spray your living areas with insecticide prior to your arrival.

RUMINATIONS

Varmints are my least favorite part of mission work, especially those that startle you with their sudden appearance on the scene. It's thrilling when Hollywood showcases them in adventure movies, but they are horrible in real life. As a child, I had an irrational fear of bugs in my bed, and I probably never completely overcame that phobia. I have minimized my dread of varmints by preparing in advance to have the upper hand in battling unwanted pests. It's also handy to bring someone along with you who is unintimidated by varmints. I traveled with one woman who was quite willing to kill cockroaches on my behalf, and the boys at the orphanage were also quite accommodating.

When it rains, insects in the tropics tend to sneak indoors. Once, I pulled down the covers of my bed and noticed lots of small bugs. I was tired and glad that I had brought along insecticide body spray, which I used on my sheets because I had no intention of sharing my bed with live bugs.

Cicada infestations are the most alarming bug intrusions because they make a loud, frightening sound. Cicadas are seasonal beetle-type creatures that lay dormant for years and then wake up in vast broods. I'll never forget waking up in the dark with a cicada buzzing around my ear. I was prepared with a fly swatter for each hand, and it did not end well for the cicada. I think I have incurable entomophobia.

1. What fears do you have to "manage" prior to committing to a Great Commission adventure?

2. What is your favorite missionary varmint story? No botfly stories allowed...wink, wink!

FIFTEEN

Beauty from Ashes

*To console those who mourn in Zion, to give them beauty for ashes,
the oil of joy for mourning, the garment of praise for the spirit of
heaviness; that they may be called trees of righteousness, the planting
of the LORD, that He may be glorified.* (Isaiah 61:3 NKJV)

When a new child is placed in an orphanage, the impact on the staff and other children is unpredictable. Yesenia's arrival and adjustment to her new home were flawless, as she blended into the group of other children with the greatest of ease. The quiet and compliant eleven-year-old girl avoided causing even a moment of grief or inconvenience for anyone. She was the classic invisible child who does not seek attention and is the last one to receive it.

Years later, in an uncharacteristic moment of self-disclosure, Yesenia told me that she often cries at night in her bedroom when no one is around to hear her quietly sobbing. The ashes began raining down upon her after the life that she once cherished went up in smoke. She was abandoned by her family, and as a result, she became an orphan.

By definition, an orphan is a child whose parents are dead, are unknown, or have permanently abandoned them. Yesenia lost her parents without anyone dying and without any closure with those she thought would love her to the end.

A few months after Yesenia arrived, I told her I wanted a photo of the two of us for a project I was planning for the following summer. Because she had been given the false and cruel impression that her stay at the home was temporary, she quickly and confidently told me that she would not be at the orphanage the next time I returned. She didn't want to stay at the orphanage. She wanted to go home to her family. She was certain that her family would come back for her, but that never happened. She was sitting in the ashes when she fully realized her parents were never coming back and that they were as good as dead to her. After a sad and lonely journey through the stages of grief, the orphanage became a replacement for her family as a trustworthy constant in her life. She grew up and became employed as a live-in adult member of the staff at the children's home.

It is rare to find a true orphan at the orphanages on Roatán. Presently, there is only one boy who fits the description at the American-owned home. A few days before Christmas one year, this boy was left as a newborn baby outside the gate of the orphanage. The gate is a considerable distance from the main house, but someone noticed a person hastily leaving a bundle and then fleeing the scene. The babe was immediately retrieved before the dogs and ants found him. He was given the name Nazareth because he was born during the Christmas season. The child has no memories of being separated from parents who didn't want him or couldn't keep him due to a court order. Nor has he been the victim of an abusive parent who betrayed their sacred trust in the various ways many of the other children have experienced.

> *The babe was immediately retrieved before the dogs and ants found him. He was given the name Nazareth because he was born during the Christmas season.*

Tía was the one constant caregiver during most of his childhood. The boy has lived his whole life in one orphanage and is unaware of what it would be like to be part of a typical nuclear family. The only true orphan at the children's home is probably the one with the most intact soul.

There are two children that I watched grow up and exit the orphanage, who suffered the scourge of abandonment even though their mother was alive and well. The mother of Nelson and Soledad dropped them off at the orphanage when they were about four and six years old. Their older sister was also dropped off at the same time, but the girl ran away and was reunited with her mother after a brief stay, which was probably planned from the beginning. After Soledad and Nelson settled into the orphanage, their mother gave birth to another child and would bring the new addition to the family on her infrequent visits. Both Nelson and Soledad struggled with lingering feelings of gloom because their mother was alive and known but rarely came to visit them. They knew she was out there somewhere, and their hearts longed for more of her. Like their older sister, they dreamed of finding their way back into their mother's heart and home.

When their mother failed to visit them for extended periods of time, the ashes of abandonment were stirred up. The siblings were despondent—especially Soledad. She appeared to be chronically depressed. The siblings wanted more of their mother, but she seldom came to give them her time and attention. Once, when their mother showed up for a visit, she used a portion of her time to take a nap instead of visiting with her children. The crumbs of affection that the mother fed her children created an unsatiated hunger for her love. The children's souls were undernourished with their diet of crumbs from an emotionally distant mother, but they never stopped begging for more crumbs.

Most likely for the benefit of Nelson and Soledad, the Lord imported a guest speaker to my church in the United States who "just happened" to be from Roatán. The man was a preacher from an impoverished area on the island where the siblings were born. It is highly improbable that the man would have been able to bankroll a trip to the United States. However, a connection made in a bizarre boating incident in the Caribbean Sea took care of that obstacle. After the incident, a complicated sequence of events took the man and his family on a journey thousands of miles away from the island to less than twenty minutes from my home. The mother of Nelson and Soledad "just happened" to attend the pastor's church back home on Roatán. Outside of the providence of God, there is no logical explanation for why the man showed up at my church against so many odds. My church is large, and I might never have met him except that he was the featured speaker one Sunday, describing his ministry and asking for volunteers to travel to Roatán on a Great Commission team.

I was astonished to hear that the guest speaker was from Roatán. I had visited the island twice, so he was of special interest to me. I listened intently to his presentation in "island talk," as it is called by those who speak the pleasant Creole English. After the church service was finished, I navigated through the crowds and found the man. The following year, we did some ministry work together in Pandy Town, and afterward, the pastor drove me to the American-owned orphanage the first year I worked there. Before he drove away, he told me that there were two children at the home named Nelson and Soledad, who were the children of one of his church members.

Knowing the man was the pastor of the children's mother, I used the connection to manipulate the situation in favor of the siblings, beginning that first year. When Nelson and Soledad expressed their sorrowful longing to see their mother, I contacted the pastor and asked him to send their mother to the orphanage for a visit. She came every time I made the request, although not always on time. Once, it looked like the promised visit was a broken promise. I couldn't stand their bitter disappointment, so the three of us were out on the main road, waiting for a taxi to take us to a nearby town to play and eat all sorts of comfort food, when suddenly, the mother showed up.

Nelson was older than Soledad and more aware of the dreadful situation in their home that had landed them in the orphanage. He struggled with extraordinary fear because of memories of violence in the home, including his father's suicide. Nelson rarely smiled. Once, when I was putting him to bed, I told him I would soon be leaving the orphanage. He asked if I would be flying home the next day. I told him that I would be staying on the island for a short vacation. He asked wistfully, "What's a vacation?"

Many of the other children at the home also had residual ashes in their lives. The ambiance of the place was heavy in spirit, and it wasn't just because it was an orphanage filled with abandoned and abused children. The ministry organization that supported the home and the children who lived there had experienced instability and turmoil during the year prior to my arrival on the scene. The orphanage had only been a 501(c) nonprofit for seven years and was not well known or supported like it is now. The home was not filled with happiness, rainbows, and unicorns. The character of the place needed a makeover.

Of course, there were no family photos on the walls, but there were no photos of the children either, with the exception of the photos of the boys and girls that were neatly posted together in straight rows and columns near the front door for cruise-ship visitors to identify who lived at the home. So, we devised a plan to make the place cozier. I asked someone to take a photo of me with every child. The next time I returned, I brought back the enlarged photos with a short love note and Bible verse to hang on the walls. We also posted photo collages of the children involved in various fun activities that we had all enjoyed together. I began this project with some hesitation because I dislike being photographed, but it paid off. After a while, I noticed other visitors doing the same thing. Most of the photos ended up posted on the bedroom walls, but the atmosphere of the place was brightened when the walls filled up with photos of the children with people who had brought beauty and joy into their lives.

The orphanage was still missing some essentials for raising happy, healthy children. The kids spent far too much time watching daytime television, and some of the shows they watched were inappropriate. However, there were no other engaging alternatives because of the scarcity of games and toys for creative play. It was especially sad to see that the infants and younger children had no quality toys to promote healthy growth and development. I knew that the typical kid back home had a surplus of such things, which made a solution doable. Back in the United States, we began collecting donations of new and used playthings. Every year after that, all members of our team carried duffle bags that were stuffed to the maximum limit with toys to encourage times of creative play and laughter.

One year, after deciding that no child should grow up without LEGOS, we asked our church members to donate any of the plastic bricks they had at home that were collecting dust. After receiving a mountain of LEGOS, we had to tell our church members to stop bringing them to us because of the weight restrictions on airline luggage. We also brought DUPLOS for the younger children.

After providing playthings, there was still a lingering spirit of heaviness at the home because the people who took care of the children on a 24/7 basis didn't have a lot of extra time to play with the kids. The children needed fun times and belly laughs to chase away the blues. So, we took them on field trips and provided other child-centered activities. Every year, we celebrated everyone's birthday at once with cake and ice cream and gifts for everyone. Twice, we arranged for an animal trainer to stop by with his domesticated capuchin monkeys, which was exceptionally fun. The man refused to take any compensation for his services, and he was kind and patient as he allowed all the children to play with the monkeys. We also did treasure hunts and find-the-minion games and toy glider plane races, with all the associated chaos that was admittedly a bit out of control.

One of our annual wild activities was moved along by everyone shouting guidance to one blindfolded child on all fours who

The kids enjoyed the scooters sent with us every year by a generous donor.

A capuchin monkey that a kind man named Alex brought to entertain the children

Enjoying frozen yogurt in West End

pounded the floor with a wooden spoon in an attempt to hit a large, upside-down stockpot with a dollar bill underneath.

James Bond Night was even more raucous. We waited until it was completely dark, and then everyone received a flashlight. We turned off all the indoor and outdoor lights. Then we had a hide-and-seek activity in the pitch black of the Caribbean night.

Trying to find and hit a big metal pot for the prize hidden beneath it

The most entertaining activity was the talent show. The boys and girls had a week to think about their various acts and the prizes for the best performances. At one of the shows, I was backstage helping the boys prepare for the mustache competition when one of the competitors decided I would enhance his act. He stuck a mustache under my nose, took my arm, and quickly led me into the ongoing talent show. Somehow, I ended up doing a difficult and crazy dance move called flossing with my partner in front of an audience that thought we were hilarious. The talent show was videotaped, so my moment in the spotlight has been preserved forever. I have a feeling it was a setup involving my team, but the fun and laughter were good medicine for our souls.

The playthings and supplies for activities take up a lot of room in our suitcases. But my favorite way of bringing beauty into the lives of the children is something that weighs nothing and takes up no space in my luggage. I always bring the children a love song. The words to the song are "I love you so much," repeated twelve times, with additional words about how the children are special to me and how happy I am to have them as part of my life. The children at the orphanage haven't heard these words enough in their lives, so they never complained about my mediocre voice. I sang it to them at night when I put them to bed. Each year when I arrive, one of them usually mentions "the song." Sometimes they start singing the song to me or they ask me to sing it to them.

One of the contestants in the mustache competition

Nelson and Soledad needed to hear the repeated message of love that the song contained. It was part of our bedtime routine. It reminded their hearts to look up to the One who had sent me to be a channel through which His love could flow to them. I loved my "tuck-them-into-bed" ministry to the children.

Most parents know that little ones need the tenderness of being tucked into bed at night for the purpose of baring their souls and bonding with a loving adult. However, you have to multiply this several times to understand the impact of this simple act when applied to abandoned children living in group homes where being tucked into bed at night rarely happens.

Nevertheless, I always dreaded going into Nelson's bedroom to tuck him into bed. He always kept his windows shut after dark, so the temperature and humidity in his room were stifling. He was too frightened to open his windows because the darkness of the cool night air revived terrifying and violent images from his childhood. I was always damp with sweat after singing the love song to Nelson. The literal meaning of the expression "blood, sweat, and tears" is a component of Great Commission work that is sometimes unavoidable.

His sister, Soledad, could be unmanageable by day, but she was a little lamb when I tucked her in at night. She made up a little routine that we followed before I sang the song. We had to finish with chatting, praying, and hugging and wait until she was tucked into bed. Then Soledad would close her eyes, begin sucking her thumb and pretend she was asleep. That was my cue to start singing, "I love you so much..." When the song was finished, I would go along with her pretense and quietly tippy-toe out of her room as though she were asleep.

Years later, as a young mother, Soledad began singing the love song to her own little ones, repeating the childhood melody that hopefully reminds her that she was also loved when *she* was a child. Maybe that's why the grown-up mother of two little girls recently told me, "Thank you so much for still loving me."

> *I wish I had a good singing voice, with perfect pitch. I do not. However, it doesn't seem to matter to the children.*

I wish I had a good singing voice, with perfect pitch. I do not. However, it doesn't seem to matter to the children. I suppose if I were a gifted singer, I might think some of the glory of singing the love song belonged to me. Without a good voice, I'm just the slightly off-key messenger. My throat usually feels a little sore after the first few nights of singing the song so many times. But my soul feels nourished to be a messenger of the Good News that the children are loved. God alone is able to raise up beauty from the ashes of trauma and abandonment, but He asks us to be His hands and feet—and sometimes His nighttime singing voice.

Young adults who have left the orphanage. The mother in the photo took the love song with her to sing to her own children.

RUMINATIONS

I've flipped several homes throughout the years as an investment. It was a lot of work, but when finished, it turned out to have been a good investment. It was an even more gratifying investment to improve the ambiance of the orphanage to make it feel less institutional and more like home.

Missionary work is a good platform for using personal strengths and skills. My own childhood was full of fun, so it was natural for me to want the same for the boys and girls at the orphanage. Some of the activities I've brought to them have been straight from the pages of my own childhood. The playthings, field trips, and activities were almost as much fun for me as they were for the kids. Laughter and fun are good sources of bonding and beauty for people of all ages.

Often, there are no skills or talents required to minister in the name of Jesus. The kids needed to hear that somebody loved them, so I sang the bedtime love song to the children with all the tenderness and sincerity I could stir up in my soul. My off-key rendition of the love song will probably be the most enduring part of my legacy to the children.

1. What life experiences have you had that give you something of value to contribute to the Great Commission?

2. How have you been the hands and feet of God?

3. How have you brought beauty into the lives of others?

Out on the field playing soccer

"...that they may be called trees of righteousness, the planting of the LORD."

Girlfriends enjoying a beach day

Fun times on the ship playground in West End

SIXTEEN

The Church in the Land of Bittersweet

When the godly are in authority, the people rejoice. But when the wicked are in power, they groan. (Proverbs 29:2 NLT)

Honduras is the land of bittersweet. The sweet children of the country have given me an appreciation for blessings I once took for granted, especially the blessing of my own wonderful parents. Once I phoned my father from a Honduran orphanage to thank him for being an available and responsible father who loved and protected me. My father passed away several years later. I'm glad I made that phone call.

Too many fathers in Honduras fail to bless their children with their presence, provision, and protection. The bitterness of that failure lands upon the heads of the innocent children. The mothers of the children also suffer as they struggle to financially support and raise children without the benefit of a father to strengthen and complete the family unit. Without the blessing of so many fathers, Honduras is not a country with a lot of happily-ever-after stories for children.

The government of Honduras has also failed the children of the country. The public schools are systemically mediocre. Educational opportunities for the children of Honduras are inadequate. The number of school days per calendar year is ridiculously low because of ongoing labor disputes between underpaid teachers and the government. Those who can afford to place their children in private schools do so because the public schools fail to provide children with what they need to break out of the prison of poverty. Children only attend school half day so the campuses can accommodate twice the student population. Some children do not attend school because their families cannot afford to purchase the required uniforms and school supplies. Children with disabilities receive little support from the public-school system. Teachers execute harsh consequences for children who misbehave in crowded classrooms. The devaluation of education within the culture of poverty adds to the problem, sabotaging the poor and discouraging them from using education as a means for upward financial mobility.

The government of Honduras has also failed to provide the children in the country with the basic needs of clean water, food, shelter, and safety. It is estimated that 10 percent of the GDP in Honduras is lost due to the high rate of crime and violence. Fractured families, drug trafficking, and gang warfare contribute to one of the world's highest homicide rates. With a population of over nine million, 66 percent of Hondurans live below the poverty line. Twenty percent of the country lives on less than $1.90 per day, mostly in rural areas. The nation has a history of natural disasters and droughts, which are devastating for agriculture in rural areas where bananas and coffee are grown and exported. Unemployment is usually three times higher than in the United States, and there is no government

One baby on Roatán was saved by missionaries, who took the child to a medical clinic because his body could not metabolize the white flour mixed with water that his mother was giving him in his bottle. She had no money to purchase baby formula.

safety net for those who cannot find jobs. Hunger and malnourishment are common, with the long-term result of stunted growth and development. At various times throughout the year, 1.5 million Hondurans are hungry.

Surviving childhood in Honduras is a bitter struggle for the poor. Some children do not have enough food to eat, and their diet is of poor quality. One baby on Roatán was saved by missionaries, who took the child to a medical clinic because his body could not metabolize the white flour mixed with water that his mother was giving him in his bottle. She had no money to purchase baby formula. Children who misbehave at home are often beaten. Older sisters are expected to share the responsibility of raising the younger children so mothers can be gainfully employed. Boys also contribute significantly to the family workload as child laborers or in other ways to help the family to survive. I have observed an interesting behavioral outcome, possibly from all the hardships that the children endure. The poor and unspoiled Honduran children that I have worked with tend to be respectful, other-centered, and grateful to be the recipient of adult kindness and attention. There is a sweetness about the way they appreciate the small things in life, and an absence of entitlement. Sadly, they have learned through beatings and deprivation that the universe does not revolve around them.

Honduras is a hopeless and unwholesome place for many children. Adequate medical care for children is mostly unavailable to poor families. Child labor is not uncommon. Honduras is one of the worst countries in the world for child abuse and sexual exploitation. There are approximately thirty-five orphanages in the country, and UNICEF estimates there are more than 170,000 orphans. Unfortunately, those numbers tell the sickening story of the vast number of children without parents who are also homeless.

The odds are overwhelmingly stacked against happily-ever-after endings for the orphans who live on the streets of Honduras under miserable circumstances. These displaced children are commonly called Resistoleros because more than half of them inhale the sweet smell of a shoe glue called Resistol, which can lead to neurological damage, kidney or liver damage, paralysis, and death. This drug of choice is a cheap and addictive inhalant used to chase away hunger pangs and emotional pains that are unbearable for children. Some of these street children are taken in by gangs, who further abuse them, hold them hostage, and force them to commit criminal offenses. One teenage boy who spent part of his life on the streets told me that he was arrested and placed in a terrifying jail for juveniles because he was caught carrying drugs in his backpack for a gang that had sheltered him on the mainland. The boy spent most of his childhood in three different orphanages, two of them on Roatán, even though his mother lived on the island only a short distance away. His father had never been involved in his life. His personal story is a good example of the brokenness of the nuclear family in Honduras and the hopeless outcome for the children.

On rare occasions, I do hear a happily-ever-after story about someone who has escaped the cycle of poverty and injustice in Honduras. Sierra's life story was exceptionally sweet. She was my next-door neighbor at a rented condo in West Bay, Roatán. Sierra, her husband, and their two sons liked to vacation on the island during their summer break, also

Sierra and her family dining on lobster in the shallow water of the Caribbean Sea

spending time with Sierra's mother. Sierra and her husband were both extroverts and sometimes brought their friends from home in the United States to join them on their summer vacations.

The friendly family probably felt sorry for me because I was alone in the condo next door. They unofficially adopted me, and I enjoyed their company. They brought me food, including some of the best tuna I've ever eaten, which went from the ocean to my plate in only a few hours. The family signed up for island tours and invited me to tag along. Together, we shared several adventures, which included circumnavigating the island, snorkeling in pristine fringe reefs, and dining on lobster while sitting on patio chairs submerged in the shallow waters surrounding an uninhabited Caribbean Island.

Back at our condo, Sierra's sweet life story came to me as a late-night blessing one evening. She is a person of many words and childlike faith in Jesus. She told me that before she lived in California with her husband and two sons, she lived in the developing nation of Honduras. Sierra described her humble beginnings as a poor Honduran girl who labored on the streets selling her mother's baked goods.

Child laborers are different than street kids and orphans. Street kids are more vulnerable than the children in orphanages, who have the security of food, education, and a roof overhead. Child laborers are somewhere in between in terms of the poverty level. Often, they live with their mother and siblings. They are common on Roatán, especially during the tourist season. Since school is only half day, they are out and about selling trinkets and food at times when children in the United States would ordinarily be in school.

Like so many child laborers in Honduras, Sierra grew up poor, without a stable father figure and without access to basics that Americans take for granted. She explained that her mother used to rise early in the morning to bake bread in a simple kitchen, and afterward, Sierra was responsible for peddling a large basket of freshly baked goods on the streets. She couldn't go home until all the bread was sold.

When I asked Sierra how she became a follower of Jesus, she told me the story of her early years as a child laborer. Although the thought of children having to work to survive is profoundly sad, the girl's unfortunate situation became her pathway to freedom. Sierra was attracted to what she described as heavenly singing coming from a church that was along the route she walked as she sold bread in her hometown. She stood in front of the church on Sunday mornings as all the potential customers were arriving for the worship services. She felt mysteriously drawn to the church for other reasons she didn't understand, but she usually missed out on the worship service because she needed to stay outside on the streets until she had sold all her baked goods. Once, the pastor of the church invited her to come inside, but she ran away because her sales that day were not going well.

Virginia Castillo's painting of a landmark church on the mainland where Sierra grew up

There were a few times that Sierra was able to join the worship service when her bread sold quickly. However, sometimes it took all day to sell everything in her basket. It didn't take long for the people at the church to figure out Sierra's work schedule. They came up with a simple plan to welcome Sierra as one of their own. Their plan was something marvelous to the young girl. Tears welled up in her eyes as she described to me what happened next. On Sunday mornings, the people in the church started arriving early to buy her bread. Not just some of her bread. They didn't stop until they had bought all of her bread in time for her to join them for worship services! So, the members of that church received freshly baked bread and a new addition to their church community. The sweet little street peddler received the Bread of Life.

Sierra's church family would later play a part in her determination to study at the university level. Higher education in Honduras is less than one hundred dollars per month, but the additional cost of transportation, school supplies, and living expenses usually excludes the poor. The church that bought Sierra's bread also helped finance her education. She told me about the miracle of God's provision for her to pay the expenses of completing the course of study for her degree. There were numerous times when she had exhausted all of her resources, and she had to trust God to provide bus money and other necessary funds to finish college. Through sheer faith and determination, Sierra became certified as a speech therapist.

Not long after finishing college, Sierra met a man who came from the United States for a friend's wedding. Sierra was a bridesmaid in the ceremony. The two fell in love, married, and bought a home together in the United States. God gave Sierra two sons, who received the sweet blessing of a devoted father. I'm not certain that Sierra will live happily ever after, but she has escaped the bitterness of Honduran injustice, and the last time I saw her, she still had enduring faith, a strong family, and summer vacations on the lovely Bay Island of Roatán.

RUMINATIONS

It's easy to miss the central point of Sierra's exceptional story. It would be wrong to conclude that her escape from the groanings of poverty and despair was rooted in her instantaneous rescue by an American man who married her and brought her to a land of abundance. Sierra's immigration to America is not the main point of the story. You have to dig deeper to discover who and what actually rescued her.

As improbable as it may sound, Sierra's humble little church rescued her. Against all odds, God used them as a powerful agent of change in a corrupt nation. First and foremost, she became a believer because the church reached out to a little girl who just wanted to put down her breadbasket and go inside the sanctuary to sing praise songs. Although she had nothing to give to the church members, they reached out to her with the Gospel and rescued her spiritually.

But the church didn't stop there. They made tangible changes to Sierra's situation as a child laborer, which was the result of the corrupt leadership in her country. When the church became Sierra's one-stop purchaser of bread, they liberated her from the injustice and burden of underage employment.

Next, the church facilitated Sierra's endeavor to attain a higher education so she could escape the misery of poverty caused by a government of kleptocrats who do nothing to enable the poor to prosper. On her own, it would have been impossible for her to finance her educational aspirations. The church enabled Sierra to break free from the unjust cultural norm that makes higher education unattainable for the overwhelming number of Hondurans living below the poverty level. The church made the impossible possible for Sierra.

Her church understood the importance of discipling Sierra, teaching her a Biblical worldview and nurturing a heart of obedience to God's Word. This saved her from drifting along with the strong current of her culture, which usually locks women into single motherhood and poverty. The church prepared her to wisely choose the Biblically defined model for her family.

The church's support of Sierra's transition from child laborer to a certificated school employee put her in a professional setting where she became associated with people who could afford the luxury of a wedding, which is where she met the groom's best friend, who married her. It was marvelous that she was able to move to the United States, but her marriage to an American was not what rescued Sierra from a life of despair.

The Body of Christ rescued Sierra from a life of despair. This accomplishment is a perfect example of the power of the Church as an agent of change in a culture where evil rulers perpetuate despair and make the people groan.

Proverbs 29:2 is a revealing commentary about the outcome of evil leadership upon nations,

The Church changed Sierra's default position of groaning under the authority of wicked rulers and instead enabled her to rejoice.

and there is no country on earth that does not have some degree of evil leadership. The Church changed Sierra's default position of groaning under the authority of wicked rulers and instead enabled her to rejoice.

Sierra's little church rescued her from a life of misery because they were a community of believers who were doers of the Word and not just hearers of the Word. The Church throughout Honduras (and in every nation on earth) would do well to follow this example and become an agent of change to rescue their citizens from the groanings of oppression and instead enable them to rejoice.

1. Read and consider the important truth of Proverbs 29:2.

2. What possible actions could the Church take in Honduras (or in any and every nation) to change the culture from groaning to rejoicing?

3. Contrast the secular notion of social justice with the Church functioning as an agent of change for the advancement of the Kingdom of God.

4. Sierra was ready, willing, and able to clearly articulate her redemption story to anyone who would listen. Write down your testimony, practice saying it, and then share it with others.

SEVENTEEN

MURDER, RAPE, AND OTHER INJUSTICES

The heart is deceitful above all things and it is extremely sick; who can understand it fully and know its secret motives? (Jeremiah 17:9)

*I*mmersion into a foreign culture rarely occurs within our comfort zone. Culture swapping tends to throw us off balance because the experience forces changes and adaptations upon us that are disconcerting. We find imperfections and injustices in other cultures that bother us. We rarely stress about the flaws in our own environment because they are our own familiar devil, but we react to other cultures with feelings of disorientation, ignorance, anxiety, and sometimes horror.

One unique mission team member out of the hundreds I've worked with in Honduras stepped into the cross-cultural experience with the greatest of ease. He was a retired Navy and Coast Guard veteran who had traveled throughout the world. He had military training that enabled him to settle into foreign territory with amazing skill and success. Prior to the start time of his first assignment on Roatán, he arrived for a reconnaissance mission. He literally put his boots on the ground and a real beret on his head for the purpose of familiarizing himself with foreign territory to better prepare for his assignment as a handyman at one of the orphanages. I was going to call him Joshua or Caleb, but we ended up calling him MacGyver, after the television character who is a brilliant problem solver, because the man fixed everything on the director's to-do list, and then he looked around for other broken things that were not on the list until the place was in ship shape.

At the time, I thought MacGyver's reconnaissance mission was silly, but the man understood something of profound importance regarding battleground strategies and preparation. He knew that when you fight a battle on foreign soil, the enemy has the home-field advantage. So, he arrived early to gather local intelligence regarding the locations and operating hours of suppliers for his handyman projects. He set himself up for success.

Prior to MacGyver arriving on the scene, I didn't understand the importance of spying out the land in order to educate myself about safety protocols and cultural differences. Ethnocentrism fools us into making the false assumption that everyone on the planet perceives the world as we do, and if they don't, it doesn't matter because they're wrong and we're right. It's easy to lose sight of the reality that we are all wrong and only God is right. We need to leave our culturally defined judgments at home and be willing to assimilate into our adopted culture with humility and a sincere value for the individuals that God has sent us to serve. We need to see them as people for whom Christ died.

In my ignorance, I had wrongly assumed that the island as a whole was much safer than the mainland. The tourist destinations on the island are much safer than the mainland, but elsewhere on the island, it is just as unsafe. There is a strong presence of government policing in tourist areas because of the huge amount of taxes generated by tourism. Also, the tourist industry implements extra security measures, including security cameras and private security guards known locally as "watchies."

I cringe when I think of some of the foolish risks I took during my early years on Roatán, doing assignments outside the safety of the tourist areas. My ignorance about the culture set me up for a number of situations that could have ended horribly. My second assignment on the island was supposed to be with a group of people from my church, but I was asked to come at a later date by myself.

It was a mistake to agree to that, especially since I was mostly left to fend for myself in a situation that was not completely safe. People sometimes tell me I'm brave to serve in Honduras. The truth of the matter is that I'm impulsive. I should have gathered more local intelligence on my first assignment on the island and done more research on the Internet before leaving home. I set myself up for failure.

I *did* check with the State Department for intelligence prior to my mission on Roatán. The website always has some sort of warning for American travelers to Honduras because of its corrupt and pathetic criminal-justice system, especially its gross failure to prosecute murderers and sexual predators. As a result of these policies, injustice abounds, particularly for women and children. The website provides the big picture of the situation on the ground, but not the smaller details that local intelligence provides, and everyone knows that the devil is in the details.

> *If you call the police, you will most likely be disappointed, which is why some criminals that terrorize communities are neutralized by vigilantes.*

When I moved beyond the boundaries of the tourist towns, I unwittingly stumbled into an alternate plane of existence where people rely on bolted doors, window bars, and junkyard dogs for security. It's not safe to go out after dark, and if you do, you cannot count on police protection. If you call the police, you will most likely be disappointed, which is why some criminals that terrorize communities are neutralized by vigilantes.

In addition to the danger of violent crime, life beyond the tourist areas is littered with land mines for women. The worst land mine for islander women is the dearth of marriage among islander couples. A prominent pastor on the island told me that about 40 percent of islander women with children do marry, but that percentage is probably inflated because he functions mostly within the context of the subculture of his church. Many of the unmarried islander women become pregnant as teenagers, which limits their opportunity to receive a higher education beyond the six years of mandatory education in Honduras. They are further disadvantaged because of the patriarchal culture that subordinates women—especially unmarried women, who do not garner the same level of respect as married women.

One of my unmarried islander friends with children posted a cartoon on social media. It showed a before-and-after scenario. The "before" cartoon drawing showed a young man passionately chasing a young woman. The "after" drawing showed the same—but very pregnant—young woman passionately chasing the same young man. It's neither funny nor fair, but it is all too common on Roatán.

Life on Roatán is hard for the multitude of single mothers. It is the perfect storm that perpetuates a multigenerational culture of poverty for women, with almost zero opportunity for upward financial mobility. Men lose out on the joy of fatherhood and also the motivation to work hard to succeed financially in order to provide for their families. Because their men fail them, women form strong bonds with other women. Grandmothers often raise the children while the mothers work, sometimes too far away for daily connection between mother and child. Single mothers who are sisters sometimes raise their children communally and, in some cases, aunts take full guardianship of their nieces and/or nephews. One mother I knew "gave away" some of her children to others who were more financially solvent in an unofficial adoption arrangement.

Because the majority of islander women give birth to their children without the benefit of marriage, the family unit on Roatán is inherently weak. It creates a never-ending cycle of misery for poor islander women. Their sons grow up without a father, which contributes to male criminal behavior and fuels the high crime rate. The net result is the Caribbean version of the wild, wild West.

Some women with children cohabitate with men in an informal union that is easily dissolved, leaving the mother with the daunting responsibility of providing for her children alone.

The net result of no higher education, no marriage, no accountability for deadbeat dads, no safe streets, and no government financial safety net is an orphan population of 170,000 children in the nation. Many of those orphans are the result of femicides. This sort of murder perpetrated by a man simply because of the woman's gender is the second leading cause of death in Honduras for women of childbearing age[1] and accounts for 9.6 percent of the total homicides in the nation. According to borgenproject.org, Honduras has earned the gruesome rank of leading the world in femicides, with a prosecution rate of just 5 percent.[2]

I should not have been shocked by the injustice when an islander woman was murdered by her former boyfriend in broad daylight in a major town because she didn't want to be with the man anymore. The attorney who told me about the crime had no confidence that the man would ever be brought to justice.

I should not have been shocked by the injustice done to two women who told me that they were raped while outside the tourist area and that they did not report it to the police because they knew it would have only added insult to injury. One of the women was a grandmother, raped by her taxi driver. Rape in Honduras is widely underreported, but the number of reported rapes, assaults, and domestic violence is still shocking. Less than 25 percent of homicides are investigated, with a 13 percent conviction rate.[3]

During my early days on Roatán, I took taxi rides alone with random drivers in places outside the tourist destinations. One time, I started out walking alone to the store because we were out of baby formula at the children's home. Then, I hopped into the cab of a truck with a perfect stranger who gave me a ride to the store. I made

---

1. Rachel Dotson and Lisa Frydman, "Neither Security nor Justice: Sexual and Gender-Based Violence and Gang Violence in El Salvador, Honduras, and Guatemala," KIND and the Human Rights Center Fray Matías de Cordova, March–July 2016, supportkind.org/wp-content/uploads/2017/05/Neither-Security-nor-Justice_SGBV-Gang-Report-FINAL.pdf.
2. Grace Arnold, "10 Facts about Violence in Honduras," *The Borgen Project*, July 8, 2019, borgenproject.org/10-facts-about-violence-in-honduras/.
3. "Violence in Honduras," ASJ, April 2020, asj-us.org/learn/honduras-violence.

it safely to the store and back to the orphanage, but I was foolish and ignorant about the potential danger of my actions. I had not done my recon like the guy in the boots and beret. If you are a woman alone on Roatán venturing beyond the well-guarded tourist sites, you need to have a repertoire of measures in place to remain safe.

I did not have safety measures in place prior to my first assignment on Roatán. I was unaware that the town where I was teaching English-language classes was not just unsafe, it was a crime epicenter. I felt safe when I stayed at the compound with other missionaries, but I had weekends off and wanted to catch a taxi to a tourist destination to play during my time off. When I walked out to the main road to find a taxi, I felt a little uneasy, so I decided to befriend two young women who were headed in the same direction. I thought if I could ride with them in the same taxi, I would be safe. Cab drivers in numbered white Toyota Corollas drive by the main road frequently, looking for customers. I was bewildered by the strange reaction of the taxi drivers when I attempted to hail a ride for the three of us. Several drivers slowed down and pulled over, but after looking at us, they drove away quickly as if we had the plague. It was weird. I was frustrated. I blurted out, "What? Do they think we're prostitutes?" Eventually, a taxi driver came along who was willing to give the three of us a ride. The women were very friendly with the man. I thought to myself, "Oh no! Maybe these women *are* prostitutes!" Our journey was like Mr. Toad's Wild Ride at Disneyland. The driver's brakes were in need of repair, so he was using the emergency brake to slow the vehicle as we traversed the winding downhill portions of the road, and he took curves too fast for comfort. I was relieved when we finally arrived at our destination, but the two women stepped out of the taxi and didn't pay the driver. They told me that it was unnecessary for me to pay the man as well. I suspected the driver exchanged his services for their services. Not wanting to be beholden to the man, I insisted on paying and tossed the money in the car window after I exited the cab.

Back at the compound, I found out that the women were twin sisters, and they *were* prostitutes. They didn't look like twins, nor did they look like the prostitutes I had seen in Hollywood productions. They did appear to be under the influence of some type of chemical substance, probably Resistol.

Early-morning devotions with hundreds of orphans at Orphanage Emmanuel

The next day was Sunday, and I tried not to look surprised when I saw the same twin sisters waving at me and inviting me to have a seat next to them at church. I had never had a prostitute for a friend, but it was sweet to have two new friends to sit with at church. Afterward, we enjoyed a free lunch that was provided as an incentive to reward locals for attending church services.

Later, I found out the lamentable life stories of the two precious women. Their father had sexually abused them most of their lives. The women were victims of a lifetime of ongoing and detestable injustice. They both ended up in a mental-health facility on the mainland. Their father is a free man known for selling his handwoven hats made of palm fronds to tourists on the beach.

Incest, rape, femicide, and sex trafficking are out of control throughout the country. There is a small but growing movement in Honduras fighting against the injustices suffered by women and children. Honduras needs major changes in the criminal-justice system so that men who harm, kill, or sexually violate women will be relentlessly hunted down and put behind bars in a miserable Honduran prison for a very long time. The nation needs a hero to rise up and be the voice for the powerless and oppressed.

None of my years of acquired intelligence regarding the victimization of women and children prepared me for the sheer horror of the sex trafficking of a child who was brought to the orphanage while I was the substitute director. The authorities brought her two-year-old sister first. The six-year-old girl came later because she was recovering in the hospital from reconstructive surgery after being raped. To make matters more intense, the orphanage director had decided to leave earlier than originally planned for rest and recuperation, so I was the only team member there when the older sister was brought by social services. Looking back, I realize I was in a providentially arranged time and place. However, at the time, it felt like I was trapped inside a hideous nightmare, and I wanted to escape.

The situation with the six-year-old girl was gut wrenching. When she arrived, she was stone faced and denied eye contact to everyone except her sister. She refused to eat. She was selectively mute and wearing a diaper. She didn't want to be touched, and when I had to clean her up in the bathtub because she had a soiled diaper, she cowered and whimpered and appeared to be completely broken and traumatized.

Oddly enough, the girl began to play with her sister and the other children after a day or two, but she refused to acknowledge the presence of adults until her aunt showed up. The aunt told me that the girl had previously been a healthy, happy child with normal toileting skills. The child's whole life had been suddenly shattered into pieces by the singular act of an evil monster.

> *Abused and abandoned, the six-year-old girl was the victim of the most brutal injustice imaginable.*

Police, lawyers, and social workers came to the home to question the six-year-old child in an attempt to assign blame for the purpose of legal prosecution. The authorities believed that the girl's mother had sold her daughter to a cruise-ship passenger. So, after being sexually assaulted by a complete stranger, the girl was removed from her home and placed in a lonely hospital for reconstructive surgery, and then more unfamiliar adults interrogated her about the worst moment of her life.

Abused and abandoned, the six-year-old girl was the victim of the most brutal injustice imaginable. The authorities did not provide a professional trauma counselor for the child. Instead, God sent a bleeding heart. I never hugged the child because she did not want to be hugged. I never had a dialogue with her because she did not want to talk to unfamiliar adults. The older girls helped me to gently attend to her needs because the girl wasn't afraid of the other children, and the older children were accustomed to helping care for the physical needs of the younger children. After about ten days, the girl and her younger sister were released into the care of their aunt. I never saw them again.

I still think about that broken little girl, and when I do, I pray for her. Sometimes I get choked up thinking about her pain. I calculate how old she would be and wonder how she is navigating life after the despicable injustice she suffered. When I considered a name to give her for writing purposes, I thought of Hagar. Like Hagar, she was also abused, abandoned, powerless, and in desperate need of safe sheltering. The experience was heartbreaking, but it was a privilege to whisper prayers over little Hagar and to softly sing her a mother's love song as she drifted off to sleep. It was a purposeful time to be on location to help provide her with a safe haven to begin the long road of recovery and healing. In my dreams, the grown-up Hagar is a godly crusader for change within the Honduran criminal-justice system and a heroic voice for the oppressed women and children of her country.

RUMINATIONS

I'm thankful that God protected me from harm during those initial years of ignorance about the dangerous situation on the streets of Honduras. Vision tours, which are short scouting trips taken by missionaries prior to their intended assignments, are a good way to gather information about safety and cultural obstacles. Whenever necessary and possible, reconnoitering an area maximizes assimilation and minimizes danger.

It has been shocking and gut wrenching to witness the fallout of injustice in Honduras. It was disturbing when I researched crime in the nation and found out that the violent injustice that I became aware of through the stories of orphan children and the women I met was commonplace. It's inexcusable that wealthy politicians in the country line their pockets with cash but fail to enact laws that would provide safe streets for their citizens, especially the most vulnerable.

My experience with the twin sisters made me wonder how a man could possibly escape punishment by the criminal-justice system after being strongly suspected of sexual exploitation for years. I didn't interact with his daughters much, but I wish I had. I'm glad they were exposed to the Gospel at the Bible-centered church we attended. I was surprised to see them in church but glad they asked me to sit with them. The church we attended tried to support the women. Their father was the one and only person who was not allowed on the church property, which may explain why the young women showed up on Sundays for services. I hope the message of hope they received in the church will someday heal and restore their souls. I wish Honduras had an effective social-service program to protect innocent women and children. I wish these women had not ended up in a mental institution. Too many life stories in Honduras do not have a happily-ever-after ending. Honduras needs the Church to do better at invading the culture in order to move it closer to compliance with Biblical standards of justice.

1. Why do politicians need to be prayed for and evangelized?

2. Why does corruption always lead to injustice?

3. Why are vision tours (or reconnaissance missions) an effective battleground strategy for missions?

EIGHTEEN

SLAYING GOLIATH

*And do not be conformed to this world [any longer with its superficial
values and customs], but be transformed and progressively changed
[as you mature spiritually] by the renewing of your mind [focusing on
godly values and ethical attitudes], so that you may prove [for your-
selves] what the will of God is, that which is good and acceptable and
perfect [in His plan and purpose for you]. (Romans 12:2)*

The ungodly injustice in Honduras evokes serious questions
about root issues and possible solutions. There are three major
institutions in the country that are out of compliance with Biblical
standards, and the result is a country that has been described as
being near the abyss. The government, the Church, and the nuclear
family are all in distress, and the country has become a disgrace
among the nations.

Honduras is a narco-state, which makes defeating the enemy
of justice at the government level terrifying to even consider. The
drug cartels reign because they traffic in terror as well as narcotics.

In 2019, the younger brother of the sitting president of Honduras
was sentenced to life plus thirty years for smuggling tons of cocaine
into the United States. His career in drug trafficking had spanned
a decade, and the prosecutors named his older brother, President
Juan Orlando Hernández, as a co-conspirator linked to the violent
drug cartels. This evil government monolith trickles down through

Protests in Honduras in 2019, held in October to demand the
resignation of President Juan Orlando Hernández

the national consciousness, creating a culture of corruption that
makes Honduras a Goliath.

The lack of justice in Honduras intensifies whenever there are
disasters like hurricanes, coups, or a pandemic. The poor always
suffer the most at these times, with widespread unemployment and
hunger and no sort of government safety net. After eight painful
years of President Juan Orlando Hernández, there was a strong
sense of despair and political malaise because of the obvious political graft of the Hernández administration. The elections that came
as Hernández was exiting center stage were more of an oppositional reaction to the status quo than a turn in the right direction.
However, the populist uprising of the people against corruption
was encouraging, as well as an election process that appeared to
be less fraudulent than the previous election. The United States
has promised billions of dollars to Central American countries to
stem the tide of corruption and impunity because of their effect
on immigration. This promise has a high probability of producing
counterproductive results, especially considering the risk of giving
foreign aid to a corrupt government for the purpose of mitigating
corruption or for any purpose.

It would be foolish to dismiss the power of the narco-state and
a government structure that empowers autocrats instead of the
people, but real solutions to the problem of injustice *are* within

the reach of the power of the Gospel, regardless of the formidable power of the government. God is infinitely more powerful than the political leaders of Honduras, and He is fully capable of advancing His Kingdom on earth, even in narco-states.

God *would* have to move a mountain to stop the breathtaking magnitude of government corruption, but isn't God famous for moving mountains? God has His eyes upon the nations, and His mercy is rich enough to convert evil political leaders and members of drug cartels. Grassroots efforts like prayer, fasting, solemn assemblies, godly political activism, and Christians obediently living out their faith could move the hand of God to change the political landscape.

> *Corrupt political leaders and violent drug cartels are not the only villains in the country—they just grab most of the international headlines.*

Corrupt political leaders and violent drug cartels are not the only villains in the country—they just grab most of the international headlines. The Church has contributed to the proliferation of injustice because it has not stood against it, nor been holy and set apart from it. Some church leaders in the country have been infected by the trickle-down influence of corruption. We expect evil politicians and drug traffickers to be unjust—not church leaders. I'm not talking about the sin of omission—I'm talking about in-your-face, arrogant injustice.

There are two Christian organizations in Honduras that I've seen up close. Both are led by nationals who are obviously compromised and should have been disciplined and terminated long ago. Instead, people wink at the corruption because this is Honduras, right? It's the familiar devil that no one is screaming about because it's been normalized within the top-down culture of corruption.

However, people tend to be uncomfortable with corruption within the Church because Jesus boldly condemned the hypocritical religious leaders of His time. That's probably why the first taxi driver who dropped me off at one of the orphanages on Roatán couldn't resist tipping me off to something that bothered him. He pointed to the ostentatious house perched up on the hill adjacent to the slum below, where the orphans lived. He explained that the man who owned the home was a prominent Baptist religious leader who used the orphanage as a means of lining his own pockets with cash from compassionate donors who want to help the orphans that live on his property.

The driver dropped me off at the curb, and I started walking toward the orphanage on the long dirt and gravel driveway. The mayor of Roatán arrived at the same time, so together we walked to the entrance of the children's home. She told me there were rumors circulating about a lack of food for the orphans, so she was there to investigate the matter. We were told by the primary caregiver at the home that the rumors were an exaggeration. She said there is always plenty of rice and beans to eat, which they buy in huge bags for the twelve boys who live there. The mayor left, having done her duty of debunking the rumor that the orphans were starving to death.

The low standard of living at the orphanage made it difficult for me to believe that the religious leader who lived in the lovely house up on the hill drove an exorbitantly priced Lincoln Navigator until I partially blocked the driveway with my cheap rental car and he started blasting his horn. The sheer arrogance of the misappropriation of funds was a sight to behold, particularly since the orphanage didn't own a vehicle. I politely moved my car out of his way, but I felt like throwing rocks.

Once, when this religious leader found out there was a leak in the roof of the children's home, he saw it as an opportunity to double-dip. He asked a donor to finance a new roof, and then requested funds from his church denomination to do the same thing.

During the delay of the roof replacement at the orphanage, the ceiling and walls in one of the disgusting bathrooms cracked and developed ugly black mold because of the leak. The bathroom needed remodeling prior to the failing roof, but now the extensive mold growth along the cracks made it an unhealthy and unsightly environment. Our team wanted the boys to have a healthier living space, so we figured out a way to finance a bathroom remodel, which was cheap by American standards. We left the money behind with the one and only trustworthy person at the orphanage whom we trusted to use the funds to complete the project instead of putting the cash into his own bank account.

The grandest of all con jobs devised by the religious leader was a trade center to teach vocational skills free of charge. Doesn't that sound like a brilliant plan for equipping poor islanders with a marketable skill to free them from the cycle of poverty? Unfortunately, it was a scam that resulted in a large three-story structure that has remained half finished for years because you can't use a completed building to swindle donors out of large amounts of money.

Stealing funds intended for orphans is bad enough, but the orphanage has had a dark history under the religious leader's authority. There are only boys living at the home now because when sexual misconduct against the girls there became too odious to ignore, they were removed. They were placed in the homes of several church members until they aged out of the poorly managed system. There is at least one islander woman who is quite vocal about the horror of growing up in the children's home. Hopefully, she and the other women know that they are heard and seen and loved by a God who takes vengeance on those who violate His moral law.

The last time I was at the orphanage, the religious leader was developing a spiritual center named after himself on the property where his home and the orphanage are located. He acts as though he is unaware of the stricter standard that he will be judged by as a religious leader. He sets the false and putrid example that you can identify as a Christian and at the same time rob orphans.

By comparison to the narco-state, the problem with the religious leader is an easy fix. God does not need to move a mountain. The Church simply needs to follow the Biblical prescription for church discipline. It *would* take courage to confront the stench of corruption because when you expose hypocritical religious leaders, it's like opening a whitewashed tomb.

Although there is a culture of corruption in Honduras that is palpable, God has a remnant of believers planted in places where the darkness only appears to eclipse His light. For example, there is a trustworthy and compassionate pastor who has been appointed to mentor the boys at the same orphanage where the corrupt religious leader is in authority. The kind pastor was born and raised on the island and has a good reputation because he is an authentic Christian who practices what he preaches. He appears to be the only adult at the orphanage who genuinely cares about the boys' spiritual and physical well-being, and they love and respect him as a father figure.

God uses people like this godly pastor to push back injustice, but there aren't enough Christian men and women like him who are willing to join the battle. Not that there is a shortage of churches and religious leaders in the country. Christianity is the primary religious preference in Honduras, at around 85 percent,[1] but this appears to have no significant effect on the flawed justice system. There is an obvious shortage of godly political leaders and police officers in this population of so many Catholics and Protestants. What would happen if devout Catholics and Protestants rose up and filled those positions of political leadership and peacekeeping?

My first visit to Central America was in 1989 with a mission team from my church. One of our Guatemalan leaders was thrilled with the gains that Protestantism had made in Central America, where Catholicism had been the dominant religion, beginning with the voyage of Christopher Columbus in 1492. When our team visited Guatemala, Vinicio Cerezo was president of the country, and he was thought to be a solid Christian. Protestants were on a roll, and they expected that the Protestant Church was going to change the face of the nation. It did not. The new converts to Protestantism did not turn their world upside-down like Paul and Silas in the book of Acts. Because the Gospel is powerfully countercultural, evangelism in Central America should have turned the culture upside-down. It

---

1. "2018 Report on International Religious Freedom: Honduras," U.S. Dept. of State, state.gov/reports/2018-report-on-international-religious-freedom/honduras/.

did not. According to some scoreboards, Protestantism has taken a slight lead over Catholicism in some regions of Central America, but it hasn't made a difference. Progressive sanctification, wherein Christians mature and develop godly character, was not a noticeable outcome when churchgoers switched denominations. The Protestant wave was obviously not a Protestant reformation because the change in church affiliation didn't significantly impact the culture.

When you consider the total percentage of Catholics and Protestants in Honduras, you have to conclude that this religious demographic must be living incognito. There is no other way to reconcile the overwhelming number of self-described believers with the off-the-charts injustice and corruption in the nation.

There are some godly Christians and churches in Honduras. The Bible-centered church that I attend on the island is a watering hole for missionaries involved in vital ministries. The pastor teaches the Bible in a way that promotes intentional Christ-like living. He encourages his flock to be doers and not just hearers of the Word. The church is involved in many outreaches to the poor and the oppressed, who are the primary victims of injustice.

Speaking up for the victims of injustice in Honduras was not what I thought God wanted me to do when I began mission work in the country. However, the toxic fallout from corruption is especially hard on poor children. After making that connection, it was natural to consider what God wanted me to do about the problem. I'm not a citizen of Honduras, but that doesn't absolve me from standing for truth and righteousness. If the pen is mightier than the sword, I can write a book. If I know bright young people who have been touched by injustice and want to do something about it, I can be an influencer. Remember my favorite bad boy on the island who turned over a new leaf? I've told him I think he would be a great lawyer. The lad certainly knows how to scream when he doesn't get his way, which might serve him well in politics.

A certificate in law is one of the three major degrees available on the island. I've asked several of the children that I've connected with at the orphanages to consider careers in law, hoping they will want to work within the legal system to push back against injustice.

I've also encouraged some of the children with the thought that they could grow up to become president of Honduras. They know that if that happens, they will have to send the presidential jet to pick me up to dine with them at the palace in Tegucigalpa, or Teguc, as the locals call it. Maybe one of the children will grow up to become the president of Honduras and bring peace and justice to the nation. Maybe one of them will become the mayor of Roatán and make sure the orphans are well fed and the religious leaders are stopped from robbing donations intended for the children.

I borrowed my grassroots idea of influencing ordinary citizens to join the fight against injustice from Tony Perkins. Honduras needs someone like him. Perhaps my favorite bad boy on the island could fill his shoes. I read Perkins's *Washington Watch* newsletters. His Honduran counterpart could publish a newsletter called *Teguc Abuse*. Like Perkins, he could put out the call for godly men and women to infiltrate the political and judicial system at every level and then equip them to go forth with the Sword of the Spirit to slay Goliath.

Sadly, there has been a dearth of leadership among godly men and women in Honduras. A portion of the Church has synchronized itself with the corrupt ethos of the nation. To some extent, Christianity in the nation resembles a subculture more than a revolutionary culture of its own, where lives are transformed from the inside out and the culture is changed to bring about justice from top to bottom.

The exhortation to be personally transformed by the power of God's Word needs to be preached so the country can be influenced and changed by Biblical standards of justice. The Church needs to go beyond evangelizing by providing sound teaching of Biblical truths, including a reverence for the blood sacrifice of Jesus. The twelfth chapter of Romans teaches about sacrificial living and the need for the faithful to resist conformity to the world.

When the nation was evangelized, some important elements of the Great Commission must have been overlooked. Included in the

Great Commission mandate were the caveats of discipleship and obedience. The logical outcome of these specifications is clearly lacking in the corrupt culture of Honduras. Instead of a tectonic cultural shift due to the large population of believers, the country earned an abysmal score of 24 out of 100 (100 being least corrupt) on the Corruption Perceptions Index of 2020. Out of 195 countries in the world, Honduras was ranked in the bottom quarter, in a tie with Zimbabwe.[2] Considering that the country has been highly evangelized, the rating is disgraceful, and there is no better descriptive considering the root word of *disgraceful*. God has *not* shed His grace upon Honduras. The Body of Christ was and is the country's most viable hope, but the lukewarmness and impurity of the Church are so out of compliance with God's Word that it would be illogical to expect God to respond with His blessing upon the land.

The brokenness of the nuclear family in Honduras can be bundled in with the failure of the Church because the Biblical model of marriage has failed to materialize. The government has contributed to the problem by making it difficult for the poor and uneducated populace to marry. N. T. Dellinger, the church father of Belize, did not accept conformity to the cultural norm of cohabitating couples who did not marry because of the paperwork and expense required to become legally married. Part of his ministry was assisting Christian couples in fulfilling the necessary paperwork and financial requirements for becoming man and wife, consequently bringing the couples into compliance with Biblical standards. It's not easy to go against the strong current of indigenous cultures, and quite often, it is frowned upon. However, the failure to comply with the Biblical standard of marriage and family has been devastating for the children and their mothers. The foundational building block of society in Honduras is made of sand.

The Church, the government, and the nuclear family in Honduras have been derailed. The Church has been a sleeping giant because the message to believe has been widely cast but the message of repentance appears to have been lost. The Christian worldview

---

2. "Corruption Perceptions Index," Transparency International, 2020, transparency.org/en/cpi/2020.

is weak in the nation. Honduras needs preachers and writers like Charles Spurgeon to wake up the slumbering Church and start a cultural revolution that will put the government and the family back on track.

Apart from divine intervention, the government in Honduras is unredeemable. Fortunately, God has unstoppable plans to destroy the injustice of sin through the advancement of His Kingdom on earth. There is hope because the heart of the president of Honduras "is like channels of water in the hand of the LORD; He turns it whichever way He wishes" (Proverbs 21:1).

Someday, God will perfectly accomplish the Great Commission in Honduras and throughout the world. Until then, He will continue to equip and send Gospel bearers to every nation. Each new laborer sent forth is one more puzzle piece in the Designer's living jigsaw puzzle. We can only imagine the celebratory chorus of heaven when the last puzzle piece is put into place, completing the breathtaking closure to the Great Commission and ushering in the Kingdom of God. Until that day, may our hearts cry out to the Lord, "Your kingdom come, Your will be done on earth as it is in heaven" (Matthew 6:10)!

RUMINATIONS

"Collective despair" is a term used by some journalists to describe the overwhelming loss of hope among Hondurans. The mood was temporarily boosted after President Hernández left office, especially when videos surfaced of the man being led away in chains for extradition to the United States on drug trafficking charges. In response to the news, social-media posts showed Hondurans celebrating outdoors and vehicles

The only true hope for Honduras is Jesus Christ, working through the Church. However, the Church as a whole has not been true to its calling, and this has driven the nation to the edge of a cliff.

caravaning boisterously through the streets. The successor to the much-hated leader, who is the country's first female president, has made hopeful promises. However, her advocacy of "reproductive rights" will only add to the despair and social injustice for women and their unborn children.

The only true hope for Honduras is Jesus Christ, working through the Church. However, the Church as a whole has not been true to its calling, and this has driven the nation to the edge of a cliff. Something went terribly wrong when the country was evangelized, with the net results of an intensely religious culture that resembles Christianity but has no Biblical moorings.

The religious leader who owns the Lincoln Navigator is a disgraceful example of the corruption in the Church of Honduras. The man is long overdue for church discipline, as well as criminal prosecution, but the situation is complicated, and the resolution would be costly. The religious leader holds the trust deed on the orphanage property, where he uses the children for personal gain. This gives him the power to shut down the orphanage at any time, which would destroy the only semblance of a family the boys have ever known. The confrontation would be unpleasant and bring embarrassment to the Church, especially since the matter has been known and ignored for years. People under the religious leader's authority would have to risk the loss of reputation, livelihood, and perhaps even personal injury in the battle for truth and righteousness.

1. Why is it necessary to confront sin in the Church and take risks for the Gospel? How have *you* gone out on a limb for your faith?

2. What transforms ordinary people into risk takers and sometimes even martyrs who are willing to die for the Gospel?

3. Will any politician or national task force be capable of resolving the outrageous government corruption, drug trafficking, and social injustice in Honduras?

4. What can the Church do to bring about a cultural shift that would diminish these three problems that plague Honduras and many other nations?

EPILOGUE

Continue to work out your salvation [that is, cultivate it, bring it to full effect, actively pursue spiritual maturity] with awe-inspired fear and trembling [using serious caution and critical self-evaluation to avoid anything that might offend God or discredit the name of Christ]. (Philippians 2:12)

Glorifying God with our lives is never going to be easy. It certainly wasn't easy for William Tyndale when he was incarcerated in a dark and dismal prison cell in Belgium for more than a year. Afterward, he was brought before the authorities and given a chance to recant for violating the law of Church and State by translating the Bible into English.

He refused.

They tied him to a stake. A rope and an iron chain were hung around his neck. The executioner was given the signal to strangle him to death by tightening the noose around his neck. Gun powder was sprinkled on the brush and wood surrounding him. Then the executioner used a torch to light the blaze that consumed the body of the man who would become the most influential person in English history.

The Church of England was determined to stop Tyndale. He was their most dangerous antagonist. His Bible translation challenged their long-standing stranglehold on power and wealth.

It was a brutal and primitive death to endure, even for someone mighty in Spirit who was prepared to lay down his life for the sake of the Gospel. For centuries, the Holy Scriptures had only been available in Latin. Translating the Bible into English or owning an unlicensed copy was considered heresy and punishable by death.

It's hard to imagine a world in which a priest would have to choose between a cruel execution ordered by the Church or remaining indifferent to ordinary people who had no Bible in their language. The historical setting was a mix of domestic and foreign affairs, not least of which was the fall of Constantinople to the religiously intolerant Ottoman Empire. The Greek scholar, Erasmus, fled to England with other religious refugees, bringing the Greek New Testament with him. When William Tyndale and other Christian intellectuals read the New Testament in its original Greek language, they were intrigued by the concept of justification by grace through faith alone. It stirred up an uneasiness about the authority and doctrines of the Church of England, which birthed the Reformation.

In addition to bringing the Greek New Testament, Erasmus brought the novel idea that "Christ desires His mysteries to be published abroad as widely as possible. I would that [the Gospels and the epistles of Paul] were translated into all the languages, of all Christian people, and that they might be read and known."

William Tyndale agreed.

Tyndale's linguistic genius made him the perfect person for translating the Bible into the language of the ordinary people of his country. It would be a complicated endeavor at a time in history when the common citizen of England was uneducated in basic English. Additionally, the English language was in an unstandardized condition, strongly impacted by German and French, and in the process of being hijacked by Latin influence. Tyndale had to determine how to retain the precise meaning of the Bible in its original languages while making his translation understandable to the ordinary speaker of a compromised language. God chose a highly gifted linguist and a man of great faith to accomplish the task with a praiseworthy degree of accuracy.

The providential timing of Tyndale's lifespan placed him in a unique time in history to become the first English Bible translator to use the printing press. He was born thirty-nine years after the printing of the first Gutenberg Bible in Germany, which launched the printing revolution in Europe. Tyndale's defiance of the law forced him into hiding from King Henry VIII and the Bishop of England. He fled to Germany, where Tyndale's English Bibles were printed and smuggled into Scotland and England inside bales of cotton. They were banned and burned in the streets by the thousands.

Tyndale's extraordinary skill as a wordsmith earned him the title of Architect of the English Language, second only to Shakespeare. His brilliant work as a translator has given us numerous phrases which are used inside and outside of Church circles. "The salt of the earth," "the skin of my teeth," and "the powers that be" are a small sampling. He also introduced new words into the English lexicon, including *zealous, anathema, scapegoat*, Passover, and Jehovah.

Joan Bridgman's analysis of Tyndale's translation in the *Contemporary Review* states, "He [Tyndale] is the mainly unrecognized translator of the most influential book in the world. Although the Authorised King James version is ostensibly the production of a learned committee of churchmen, it is mostly cribbed from Tyndale with some reworking of his translation."[1]

Although Tyndale attained advanced literacy skills in at least seven languages by the age of twenty-two, he had the humble heart

---

1. Joan Bridgman, "Tyndale's New Testament," *Contemporary Review* 277, no. 1619 (2000): 342–46.

of a servant. He was known to take weekly breaks from his workload of Bible translation to minister to religious refugees and the poor and also to read the Bible to others in their native tongues. His personal writings stated, "My part be not in Christ, if my heart be not to follow and live according as I teach." Although he was imperfect, like all humanity, his reputation as a follower of Jesus remains untarnished.

His servant's heart would be his undoing. A man named Henry Phillips gained Tyndale's friendship and confidence with evil intent. Phillips shared meals and the reading of God's Word with the fugitive Bible translator. Phillips ultimately lured Tyndale away from the safe confines of his residence and delivered him into the hands of soldiers, much like the betrayal of Jesus by Judas Iscariot.

Not many men or women have William Tyndale's skill set, but the Bible is full of stories about ordinary people that God used in magnificent ways. Some of the men that Jesus chose as His disciples were commercial fishermen who would become the first disciple makers.

The unspoken problem is that ordinary people are normally reluctant to commit to a transformed lifestyle that would make them unwanted agents of change. Additionally, we don't readily build Biblical disciplines into our lives that would support the development of spiritual maturity against the pushback of our corrupt nature. We are more inclined to choose comfort and indulgence than the sort of sacrifice and suffering William Tyndale chose.

How then are we able to glorify God with our lives when it's entirely unnatural to do so? The New Living Translation gives the simplest answer in Philippians 2:13 with these words: "For God is working in you, giving you the desire and the power to do what pleases Him." God sets us up for success. He is an equal-opportunity Father, commanding all His children to receive the desire, power, and privilege to make His name known as participants in the Great Commission. The window of opportunity for this offer begins the day we are born spiritually and expires the day we die physically. We are left on earth during this time span for the purpose of telling the unredeemed where redemption is found and then discipling them in the faith. William Tyndale decided to make the name of Jesus known to English speakers everywhere. He used what he had as an offering to God, and we can do the same.

After being redeemed and justified by faith in Jesus, the journey toward spiritual maturity is sprinkled with trials and tribulations, supported through discipleship, and enabled by the Holy Spirit. Philippians 2:12 gives the instructions for growing in the faith, exhorting believers to "continue to work out your salvation [that is, cultivate it, bring it to full effect, actively pursue spiritual maturity] with awe-inspired fear and trembling [using serious caution and critical self-evaluation to avoid anything that might offend God or discredit the name of Christ]." This is the prescription for our part in reining in our corrupt natures in order to unleash the process of progressive sanctification.

Spiritually mature believers who emerge from this process do not blend into the world. They become dangerous to the existing social order, as the power of the Gospel within them invades the culture. Tyndale worked out his salvation with fear and trembling. The process transformed his life and powerfully changed the English-speaking world with the active and living Word of God. His life work as a Bible translator made him an extraordinary influencer with a legacy that continues in every English-speaking country in the world. The way he lived out his faith and then laid down his life for the furtherance of the Gospel was like a stunning masterpiece that magnified the Lord.

The translation of the Bible into Spanish for ordinary people has had a similar history with the same questionable opposition from the Church. Unfortunately, the most widely used Spanish translation in Latin America does not have similar acclaim for retaining the precise meaning of the Bible in its original languages. In any case, it was telling to come across a written observation in an article entitled "Gospel Light in Honduras," which stated, "Bibles are plentiful, but books presenting sound theology are rare."[2]

---

2. Dennis Roberts, "Gospel Light in Honduras," The Gospel Coalition, March

It is self-evident that the Biblical prescription for progressive sanctification was not picked up and swallowed when the Gospel was dispersed in Honduras. This is particularly obvious in the governance of the nation. But even within the Church, there are obvious inconsistencies with Biblical doctrines, which should be surprising in a nation where the overwhelming majority of the population identifies as Christian.

Honduras is not the only country that has been evangelized without faithful adherence to the basic tenets of the Great Commission, but it is one of the best examples. According to the Corruption Perceptions Index, people do not think of the rule of law and honorable leadership when they think of the highly evangelized nation of Honduras. They think of unsafe streets and kleptocrats.

In 2022, Juan Orlando Hernández, the former president of Honduras, was arrested, extradited to the United States, and indicted on drug trafficking and weapons charges. It was unbelievable because blatant corruption with impunity is commonplace in the nation. The charges in the indictment are shocking and include murder, machine guns, and a million-dollar bribe from El Chapo himself that helped Hernández buy the presidency. Without a doubt, the ex-president will be convicted and incarcerated for the rest of his life, sending a clear message to the other corrupt politicians in the nation to commit their evil deeds more stealthily. The United States Department of Justice is never going to make a significant difference in the deep and wide culture of corruption in Honduras. That's the responsibility of the Church.

But like a stone skipping upon the water, the casting of the Gospel in Honduras has repeatedly impacted the surface of the culture and then dropped beneath the public consciousness. The nation has been a mission failure that requires the attention of church leadership for the purpose of analysis, a plan for resolution, and restoring methodologies for evangelism to Biblical settings, including expanding what we think of as spiritual and imbued with eternal meaning in this life. Community ethics, political representation,

---

20, 2015, thegospelcoalition.org/article/bringing-gospel-hope-to-honduras/.

civil law, our vocations, family government, business ethics, and church all serve as our training ground in developing a well-rounded godliness that will influence society.

May the Lord purify the Church and ordain laborers who are mighty in Spirit to faithfully implement the Great Commission worldwide, creating a masterpiece that showcases God's glory.

> So then, my dear ones…, continue to work out your salvation [that is, cultivate it, bring it to full effect, actively pursue spiritual maturity] with awe-inspired fear and trembling [using serious caution and critical self-evaluation to avoid anything that might offend God or discredit the name of Christ]. For it is [not your strength, but it is] God who is effectively at work in you, both to will and to work [that is, strengthening, energizing, and creating in you the longing and the ability to fulfill your purpose] for His good pleasure. (Philippians 2:12–13)

Amen.

Please feel free to reach out to me at: theladyonthebridge@gmail.com.

ABOUT REBECCA FRIDAY

*R*ebecca Friday has lived in the Golden State since before her second birthday. She was born the third of four children to a couple from the Midwest. Her father was born at home on a farm to a sharecropper but rose to a management position in the aerospace industry, specializing and collaborating on thrust chambers that were used on NASA's Apollo as well as the first four Space Shuttle projects.

Rebecca graduated with honors from California State University, Northridge, and also earned a TESOL certificate from UCSB (Teaching English to Speakers of Other Languages). She has worked in both the Christian and public school systems, with experience as a regular classroom instructor and also as an English Language Development Resource Teacher.

Rebecca became a Christian as a teenager. She has been married for more than fifty years, with three children and five grandchildren.

She started making short-term missionary trips in the eighties, completing twenty-four trips to Latin America as of the publication of this book. Her role as a missionary team member has been as an English-language teacher, kitchen manager, and substitute orphanage director.